All enquiries should be directed to the author's email:
hi@iamadedoyin.com

ISBN : 9781728963679

Edited by Pamra

Book Cover Design by Freepik

Published on Amazon

For more information kindly visit – www.iamadedoyin.com/betechpro

CONTENT

CONTENT

CONTENT

Dedication

This book is dedicated to David Mosimabale - a silent champion, world changer and a true reformer. Your labour of love - Empowerment Series led hundreds of us on the path of positive personal transformation. This book is the fruit of the selfless seeds you planted years ago in Federal University of Technology Akure (FUTA).

Acknowledgement

Special thanks to Almighty God for the gift of life, grace and knowledge to make this book a reality. To my parents, Mr. and Mrs. Adedeji, thank you for your devotion and the sacrifice to make Sade, Toun and I the adults we are today. A happy family is everything; special shout out to my uncles, aunties, cousins, in-laws, nephews and nieces - space will not allow me to mention you all by name. I love you all.

Church plays a huge role in my personal growth; thanks to Pastor E. A. Adeboye, Pastor Bola Odutola, Pastor Tope and Kemi Abe, Pastor Tunji Adeyinka for your spiritual guidance and being positive role models. Pastor Wale Akinyanmi, thank you for being a good mentor.

True friends like Dupe Abifarin Dosumu are rare; you were that friend that believed and cared enough about my writing back then in secondary school, those little actions of yours are part of the reasons writing will always be one of the feathers I have added to my cap. Philip Agboola, thanks for your support at one of my most challenging moments; it was during that period that I had the idea for this book. Bukola Mabel Richard there is so much I would have loved to say but I can't find the right words, thanks for the true and selfless friendship.

David Mosimabale and Yomi Babatola of CCF NIFES thanks for providing positive directions that transformed my story. Segun Adelaja, Damola Adeagbo, TJ and all the Khrome Konsult folks, thanks for the platform to learn, to start my journey into tech and meet a lot of awesome people. The memories of Khrome Konsult remain special to me; how FUTA's student union building became the centre of creativity, innovation and possibilities.

To Patience Omeruo, thank you for taking out time to go through this book.

Finally, I want to thank Mr Rotimi Arowa and Olaoluwa Laniya of 2807 Studios for the work that went into the design and printing of this book.

Graphics in this book are designed by Freepik and Flaticon.

Foreward

"Where do you see yourself in five years?"

Interviewers often pose this question to get a better sense of your passion and aspirations.
Friends and family ask this question because the big picture is more likely to paint an accurate view of what you want to pursue.

It's funny, I'm just over my five-year mark out of college, so I guess I'm at the perfect crossroads to reflect and anticipate the next half-decade to come.

If you asked my undergraduate-self, I wouldn't have given you an answer anything close to what I'm doing now.

In 2007, I entered New York University as an ambitious freshman, eager to make my mark and become a journalist. I knew I found a thrill in digging for stories and learning to empathize with others from very different walks of life. I loved waking up to the Sunday morning paper and dreamt of seeing my name in one of those bylines one day.

In 2009, one of my journalism professors required the class to create Twitter accounts and learn to use social media to promote our stories. Facebook was still a private platform back then, and barely anyone used it to share news. But Twitter was a whole different universe. It was fast-paced, and it provided an outlet to connect with people and to discover stories in real-time.

That was the early beginnings of what led me to a career in digital marketing. Since then, I've driven a range of digital marketing programs. I've done email marketing, content marketing, social media -- you name it.

Fast forward five years and I'm a Product Marketing Manager for a company that builds emerging tech, like IoT, VR/AR, and AI. My core passions remain the same, but my day-to-day looks really different now than what I imagined six years ago. I still dig for stories, but for customer stories of needs and pain points.

My job is to find the specific intersection between customer need and product value. I help customers get more out of the product by prioritizing features that align with their pain points and workflows.

I find it incredibly fulfilling, solving problems and seeing concepts go from the whiteboard to the market. And even when I'm "off the clock," I find myself thinking of new solutions to help things run just a little bit smoother.

Foreward

That's why when I receive the five-year question now, I keep it vague. I say, "I see myself continuing to learn and build."

The fact is, technology is evolving at an incredible rate, and it would be a disservice to our future selves to a set a path based on the limited view we have today.

The software, the hardware, the platforms we're communicating on today -- they'll all be radically different in five years, which means our jobs will be too.

All this isn't to say that asking the question, "Where do I see myself in five years?" is not useful. I think it's important to be forward-thinking and to be curious. Asking questions is great for growth. That's why you're here, after all. You have a general interest in tech, but you're curious how to apply that in real life.

As you pursue this new journey, whether you're just graduating from college or you're making a career switch, I hope you never lose this curiosity. Don't stop asking about the future, but also don't feel pressured to stick to your answer.

There are many different ways to fulfill your passions and pursue meaningful work.

You're already well on your way with this book. Happy reading!

Denise Chan

Denise Chan is a digital storyteller with six years of experience helping early-stage startups build, brand, and grow their businesses. She is passionate about creating things that make life just a little bit easier for brands and people. Denise is currently a Product Marketing Manager working on emerging tech products such as IoT, AI, and VR/AR. Prior to her current role, she ran content at Bitly and Mailjet and founded Gramforacause, an influencer marketing agency for non-profits. You can find her on Twitter at **@denisechan26** and Instagram **@withlovedc**.

Introduction

hange is constant, and the impact of change on humanity is evolving. As time fades away and change occurs, humanity continues to evolve. The concept of an era is one way we try to make sense of our continuous evolution. From the Stone Age to the Industrial Age, and now the Information Age, humans have always found new and exciting ways of doing things and fixing problems.

It is no doubt that our present era, the age of information, is the best time to be alive. In this era, technology is not simply part of human evolution; it is becoming a major driver. It is part of our daily living. Everywhere you turn to, technology plays a significant role. We have smartphones that can perform almost any function. Smart homes that can detect intruders, smoke, temperature, and even make decisions. We have smart offices today where everything works without papers. Smart cars are the next revolution in the automobile industry. We also have smart power grids that control how we use power. A lot is changing around us to enhance our existence.

Beyond this, technology is helping us reach new heights and explore new possibilities. We are exploring new territories and further pushing back the boundaries of impossibility with technology. Access to information is now as simple as pushing a button. Never in the history of humanity have we had so much information available to us. Information is power and we can access that power. You can access almost any information you need.

New and exciting career options are opening up every day in the technology space. Every profession today relies on technology in some ways to achieve better results. One thing is clear; the future of work is technology. The best jobs of tomorrow will be jobs integrated with technology. So, build your career path around technology and watch the opportunities it will open you to.

Going through this book, you will gain insights into what it takes to build a career in the tech industry. It will help you explore the tremendous and exciting opportunities available in technology. It will also guide you to understand your personality and which tech career choice will be best for you.

For Tech trainings,videos and resources

Visit : www.iamadedoyin.com

Join or follow the conversation with the hashtag

#BeTechPro

SECTION 1

UNDERSTANDING TECHNOLOGY

ICT Demystified

In talking about technology, two major words used to describe the industry are IT or ICT. IT means Information Technology while ICT means Information and Communication Technology. However, IT doesn't cover the full scope of what the technology industry is about. Information Technology, IT, tends to cover the hardware and software used for business. This includes digital devices, computers, software, servers, data centres and computer clusters, used to process and manage information. ICT has a broader coverage of the industry's scope of work. ICT includes Information Technology, telephony, mobile, wireless networks, the content (text, audio, video) you generate using IT tools and the entire business around technology. In the industry, we prefer using IT although it is more of a subset of ICT.

A good definition of ICT is found on Wikipedia :

Information and Communications Technology (ICT) is an extended term for Information Technology (IT) which stresses the role of unified communications and the integration of telecommunications (telephone lines and wireless signals), computers as well as necessary enterprise software, middleware, storage, and audio-visual systems, which enable users to access, store, transmit, and manipulate information.

Let's try to break ICT down further:

I – Information: This represents the contents created using technology. These include text, audio, videos, visuals and data.

C – Communication: This is how we pass on information using technology. It is the flow of content and connection with people across the world in different locations at any given time.

T – Technology: This is the engine room that brings information and communication together. Technology provides the tools to generate content and the platform to transmit the content across the world.

These three aspects come together to define what the technology industry is about.

The Next Tech Revolution is Here

When the internet emerged in the early 90s, businesses saw the huge potentials it could bring. Within a short time, we witnessed rapid expansion in the usage of the internet. This ushered us into a new era – the Information Age. The information age changed how we live, communicate and transact business. It opened humanity to a new realm of possibilities and interesting opportunities. The innovations fuelled by the internet have changed what our mobile devices can do. Today, smartphones are as powerful as computers and can do almost anything we need them to do. With millions of mobile apps out there, the possibilities are almost endless.

Humanity is beginning to witness the next wave of revolution - a digital revolution. We are standing on the edge of a revolution that will completely change humanity. This revolution would bring together the physical, digital and biological world. It will create new systems, possibilities and solutions. It will have a significant impact on individuals, the global economy, industries and governance.

The internet brought us to the information age and mobile revolution. New technologies like artificial intelligence, the Internet of Things, robotics, self-driving vehicles, nanotechnology, 3D printing, blockchain, quantum computing and Virtual/Augmented reality are ushering us into the next era. This will be an era where changes in our culture, society, economy and governance will be at the speed of thoughts. An era where technology will not only be part of our lives, it will be our lives. An era where technology won't merely help us with work, it will do the work. Homes will be internet enabled thereby changing the concept of family. Transportation will be automated, humans will work alongside intelligent robots and computer artificial intelligence will make more decisions. The possibilities and opportunities of tomorrow's world are exciting and endless.

Professor Klaus Schwab, Founder and Executive Chairman of the World Economic Forum, describes this era: *"The new technology age, if shaped in a responsive and responsible way, could catalyse a new cultural renaissance that will enable us to feel part of something much larger than ourselves – a true global civilization... We can use the Fourth Industrial Revolution to lift humanity into a new collective and moral consciousness based on a shared sense of destiny".*

The Future of Work

At the centre of the future of work is technology. Rapid advancements in technology are reshaping our human experience. Advanced technologies like mobile technology, Internet of Things, robotics, cloud computing, big data, renewable energy, shared economy, automation, biotechnology, 3D scanning and printing, virtual and augmented reality, and blockchain are creating new possibilities and experiences around us. These technologies are helping to push back the boundaries of limitations and enter new territories.

As the information age ushers us into the next digital revolution, the fundamental nature of work and how we transact business will once again change. New technologies will disrupt old business models and bring forth new models. These new business models will need new skills and make changes in the structure of the workforce. While some jobs will be lost to the coming digital revolution, new jobs will be created. These jobs will be less physical and more technical. Let's take delivery services for example. Today, delivery companies need vehicles and drivers to deliver their products to customers. With the growth in drone technology, there won't be a need for drivers anymore. Drone operators will manage and control the operation of fleets of delivery drones. Recently, Rwanda began to use drones to deliver medical supplies to remote hospitals. The results of this project are interesting. While delivery by road may take a day, it takes less than one hour for the drones. Each drone can make about 150 deliveries every day. Drones and drone operators will deliver better results.

According to a recent report by the World Economic Forum, "65% of children entering primary school today will end up working in completely new job types that don't exist yet". New job roles are opening up while old job roles are fading away. Understanding the coming global changes will make it easier to prepare for them and it does not take so much to understand. By paying attention to changes around you and reading up about them, you will be able to transition from old obsolete jobs to newer ones. The scope of jobs and employment is changing and we owe it to ourselves to prepare for these changes.

The smartest move to make is to prepare for the future of work. You can prepare by learning about the changes in your chosen field and tailoring your career development towards it.

The future of work holds a lot of promises but only for those whose minds are open to the changes that digital technology brings.

For Tech trainings,videos and resources
Visit : www.iamadedoyin.com
Join or follow the conversation with the hashtag
#BeTechPro

SECTION 2

GETTING TO KNOW YOURSELF

It Starts with Passion

"Choose a job you love and you will never have to work a day in your life." – Confucius

The first major step to be the tech professional you dream of becoming is PASSION.

Do you have a passion for technology?

Before you answer, think about this. If you have the opportunity to go on a weeklong vacation, would you get bored working on computers and gadgets all through the week? No doubt, being a tech professional is one of the coolest careers. People consider them very smart, intelligent and usually well paid. You also get to use technical terms to impress and sometimes, confuse people. Yet, beyond the glamour, a career in technology can be long, tedious and lonely. It requires a lifetime of continuous in-depth learning because technology evolves at a very fast pace. 80% of what would keep you on top of your game and make you one of the best players in the tech industry is self-learning. You can't embark on a lifetime journey of self-learning without passion. If you decide to come into this industry for the wrong reasons, you won't be able to able to keep up with the pace of the industry's evolution. You will get fed up and switch career. I have seen people who came into the industry for the wrong reasons such as money or glamour; today, many of them have switched to other career paths. It is also important to understand where your passion lies within the industry. For example, you may love to play around with cables and fix electronics. A good career option for you would be hardware support, networking, data centre building and management. If you decide to go into User Interface designs because you have a friend who designs User Interface (UI) for web-based software and gets paid a lot, you will struggle to be the best. This happens because the path you chose is not your natural place of strength in the technology

7

industry. Find your place of natural strength, develop it and stay focused.

Trust me; there is nothing more rewarding than building a career around something you are passionate about. It has a huge positive impact on your family, health, physical and spiritual state.

Why is passion so important in career choice especially in the technology industry?

What type of adult do you want to be?

One that wakes up every morning upset about work, tired of showing up for work daily but have to because you have to provide for your family.

Or

One that wakes up every morning keen about work, quitting is not on your mind because you are doing exciting things at work.

Let's take a quick overview of life after school. As a working adult, you will spend approximately 9 hours at work and 5 hours with your family. You will most likely spend 7 hours resting and 3 hours carrying out other activities. So, in a week you will spend approximately 45 hours building your career. The important question you should ask yourself is this. Do you want to spend 45 hours weekly as an adult doing something you don't like or having fun? When you devote your life to what you are passionate about, it is no longer a job. IT IS FUN. Don't forget that the 9 hours spent each day at work will influence how you will spend the 5 hours with your family. It will also determine how well you sleep for the 7 hours at night. You owe it to yourself to make a commitment to turn your passion into a career.

Your passion should be something you enjoy doing anytime and naturally at ease with. Take some time to research career options relating to your passion and develop as a professional in that career.

- Do I belong to the technology industry?
- Do I have what it takes to build a successful career in the technology industry?

Only you can answer those questions by looking inwards, figure out the things you enjoy doing. Let those thoughts light up a burning desire in you to do great things using technology. Find a career path that matches that burning desire and you are on your way to becoming a tech professional. If those thoughts can't spark a burning desire in you, then the technology industry may not be your place.

Personality Assessment

Passion is an important factor in deciding if you belong to the technology industry. Understanding yourself and your personality type is also very important. The hard truth is that you cannot deny who you are. Your personality type goes a very long way to determine which career path suits you. Understanding your personality will help you find what you like to do. This will make you happy, successful and fulfilled. Happiness and fulfilment will make you a better adult; you will have a great family and live a richer life.

If you got to this chapter, I assume you are passionate about being in the technology industry. We will now explore the different personality types and how it affects your choice of an ICT career. To unlock who you are, you must go on a journey of self-discovery and be truthful to yourself.

Quick personality assessment for you

- Answer these questions truthfully.
- There are no right or wrong answers.
- Each of the four questions has two answers. You have to choose one and write down the letters before the answers you chose.

Are you ready? Let's do this….

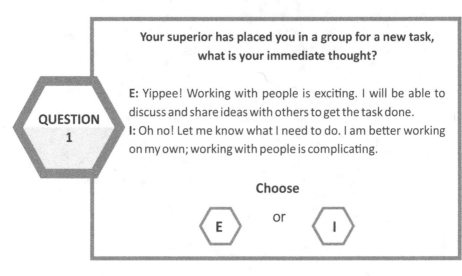

Your superior has placed you in a group for a new task, what is your immediate thought?

QUESTION 1

E: Yippee! Working with people is exciting. I will be able to discuss and share ideas with others to get the task done.
I: Oh no! Let me know what I need to do. I am better working on my own; working with people is complicating.

Choose

E   or   I

QUESTION 2

New clubs have been created in your school and you have to choose, which would you likely join?

S: History, Statistics Club
N: Arts, Creative Club

Choose

S or N

QUESTION 3

Your close friend just returned your computer and it is broken. How would you feel?

T: I am angry, I have to be told how it happened. I need to know if my friend was careless with it.
F: I am unhappy but it is ok. People usually make mistakes.

Choose

T or F

QUESTION 4

How do you prefer to work?

J: I prefer a structured workplace where rules and deadlines are important and there are proper plans and instructions on what to do.
P: I prefer flexibility, rules and deadlines should be flexible. I love surprises because it brings new situations which make me solve problems on the go.

Choose

J or P

I believe you answered the questions truthfully and now have FOUR letters. Keep those letters; it is the key that we will use to unlock who you are in the next chapter.

Unlock Your Personality

Over the last decades, several studies and research have gone into helping people understand their personality type. These studies and research provide a wealth of data and information on how who we really are can have an impact on the type of work we like to do and the environment that brings out our productivity. This ultimately provides a direction for our career choices.

In this book, we will be focusing on one of the most popular frameworks for personality identification-The Myers-Briggs Type Indicator® (MBTI®). The MBTI® is a non-judgmental approach to helping individuals identify their strengths, preferred environment, their inter-human connection level, gifts, decision-making pattern and their preferred private life.

The Four Characteristics of Human Personality Type

Note: There is an element of both in everyone but we are more comfortable and naturally want to be in one of the two.

INTERACTION TYPE

How do you interact with the world around you?

Are you external and action-oriented (extrovert) or internal and reflective oriented (introverts)?

If you :	If you :
1. Like working with other people or a team 2. Like a lot of activities in a busy and fast-paced environment 3. Think out loud and ask questions 4. Are talkative, outgoing and enjoy the attention.	1. Are reserved and private 2. Prefer working independently or with a small group 3. Prefer calm and quiet spaces 4. Think things through in your head 5. Don't like attention
You are most likely to be :	You are most likely to be :
E **Extroverts**	**I** **Introverts**

INFORMATION INTAKE

When you interact with the world, how do you process the information?

Do you like dealing with reality, data, facts and figures (sensors)?

Or do you prefer imagination, creativity, abstract, ideas and concepts (intuitive)?

If you :	If you :
1. Like focusing on data, facts, history and figures 2. Like to use past experience to make sense of the present 3. Prefer ideas that have real-life applications 4. Are interested in details	1. Like creativity, new ideas, innovation and possibilities. 2. Are more drawn to new and abstract things 3. Prefer to explore new ideas and ways to solve problems 4. Easily get bored and impatient with too many details
You are most likely to be :	You are most likely to be :
S **Sensors**	**N** **Intuitive**

3

Decision-making Style

When the world provides you with information, how do you process it and make a decision?
Do you make decisions based on available facts, logical analysis and objectivity?
Or do you base it on emotions, personal values and compression?

If you :
1. Prefer to make decisions based on facts, logical analysis and objectivity
2. Are you a strong believer in fairness and justice
3. Carefully weigh options before making a decision

You are most likely to be :

T
Thinkers

If :
1. You prefer to make decisions based on emotions, personal values and compression
2. You are generally sensitive, understanding and forgiving
3. Your decision making is subjective because you are sensitive to how your decision will affect others

You are most likely to be :

F
Feelers

4

Organisation Style

Are you comfortable with organisation, following rules and directions?
Do you prefer to have a solid plan and are tolerant to routine (judgers)?
Or do you prefer spontaneity, flexibility and don't mind a bit of chaos?
Rule and routine isn't your thing (Perceivers).

If you :
1. Are comfortable with proper organisation, rules, routine and deadlines
2. Always prefer detailed plans of what to do and strictly follow instructions
3. Like to be sure of what you are getting into.

You are most likely to be :

J
Judgers

If you :
1. Find too much organisation, rules and routine boring
2. Prefer flexibility in rules and deadlines
3. Love uncertainty, spontaneity and makes decisions on the go
4. Don't mind chaos, surprise and easily adapt to changes

You are most likely to be :

P
Perceivers

Pick up your four letters and review them again. This will help you understand your personality type better.

Discover the Perfect ICT Career for You

You can review the table below. Match your personality type with the Ideal ICT career choice for you.

PERSONALITY TYPES	IDEAL ICT CAREER CHOICE
ISTJ	Database Administration Computer Support / System Admin Technology and Online Marketing Telecoms Engineering Data Analyst
ISFJ	Customer Service
INFJ	Photography Content Writer
INTJ	Software Developer Mobile App Developer Web Designer / Developer Artificial Intelligence
ISTP	Media, Content and Communication Cyber Security Computer Networking and Architecture Computer Support and System Admin Telecoms Engineering Geographical Information System

13

PERSONALITY TYPES	IDEAL ICT CAREER CHOICE	
ISFP	Visual Effect (VFX) Cyber Security	
INFP	Digital Graphic Design Photography Game Development Visual Effect (VFX) User Experience Designer (UX) User Interface Design (UI) Video Editor	
INTP	Media, Content, Communication Software Developer Mobile App Developer Web Designer / Developer	
ESTP	Video Production Media, Content, Communication IT Project Management Cinematography Geographical Information System	
ESFP	Customer Service	
ENFP	Photography Music production Computer Aided Design	

PERSONALITY TYPES

IDEAL ICT CAREER CHOICE

PERSONALITY TYPES	IDEAL ICT CAREER CHOICE	
ENTP	Video Production Media, Content, Communication Computer Aided Design Web Designer / Developer Cinematography	
ESTJ	Business System Analyst Technology and Online Marketing	
ESFJ	Tech Trainer Customer Service	
ENFJ	Photography Media, Content, Communication	
ENTJ	Web Designer/ Developer Software Developer Mobile App Developer	

NOTE:

The table above is meant to be a guide especially for starters. You still have to review these career options and decide what you want to do.

For Tech trainings,videos and resources

Visit : www.iamadedoyin.com

Join or follow the conversation with the hashtag

#BeTechPro

SECTION 3

LET'S EXPLORE ICT CAREER OPPORTUNITIES

Digital Literacy

The pathway to a rewarding career in technology starts with digital literacy lessons which include an introduction to computing, basic digital graphics, using the internet and computer hardware. Most computer training centres around offer this training; be careful enough to pick a good one. You can ask people around you for a good computer training centre.

Any computer training centre you decide to go to should take the following courses:

1. A general introduction to computers. This will include the history of computer and the various parts of the computer.
2. An understanding of computer hardware and software. This will include the difference between input and output devices with examples.
3. An understanding of the Microsoft's Windows Operating System, Apple's iOS or Linux. Most training centres use Microsoft's windows Operating System. It easier to learn and understand. You should familiarise yourself with any of these operating systems.

4. The use of the Microsoft Office Suite which comprises :

- Microsoft Office Word – This is generally used for typing and printing documents. It is used for manipulating text-based documents. It is the electronic equivalent of paper, pen, typewriter, eraser, and the dictionary and thesaurus.

- Microsoft Office Excel - This is a spreadsheet software used to enter data in tabular form. It uses rows and columns of cells; each cell can hold text or numeric data or a formula that uses values in other cells to calculate the desired result.

- Microsoft Office PowerPoint- This is used for making business presentations.

- Microsoft Office Access- This is a database software. A database is any collection of data organised for storage in a computer memory and designed for easy access by authorised users. The data may be in the form of text, numbers, or encoded graphics.

5. Once you have mastered the use of the Microsoft Office Suite, you can now go ahead to learn the following depending on your interest:

1. Internet usage, web browsers, search engines, emailing and social media platforms.

2. Hypertext Markup Language (HTML) for basic website design.

3. Digital Graphic Design using Corel Draw, Photoshop and Adobe Illustrator; you can create your own handbills, posters, wedding and event invitations etc.

6. Computer hardware and basic networking.

Take some time out to develop your newly acquired skills. Get comfortable with the use of the computer. Then it is time to take that GIANT LEAP and get your first set of professional ICT certifications. Some popular entry-level certifications you can consider are:

- IC3 Digital Literacy Certification - www.certiport.com
- Microsoft Digital Literacy - www.microsoft.com/en-us/DigitalLiteracy
- CompTIA A+

Digital Graphics Design

Do you have a passion for colours, shapes and patterns? Digital graphics might just be the career path that suits you. A digital graphic art designer or graphic designer creates visual concepts with colours, shapes, images and patterns. A graphic designer uses computer graphic software like Adobe Photoshop, Adobe Illustrator, Adobe InDesign, Corel Draw Graphic Suite to develop layouts and designs for the production of magazines, banners, logos, business cards, greeting and promo cards, posters, brochures, advertisement items, branded items and other visual items. At the centre of this career is communication. Any item the graphic designer creates is to communicate a message to an audience. So, the more effective your designs are in doing this, the greater your chance for growth. Generally, graphic designers should be good communicators. You need to understand a client's need by asking the right questions. You also need to create a creativity roadmap for every graphic job you have to do. The design industry is very dynamic, so graphic designers should be continuous learners. Let your passion and drive fuel your learning process.

As a graphic designer, you will likely spend more time working with advertising, promotions, and marketing managers, creative directors, publishers and printers, industrial designers, multimedia professionals and web developers.

Adobe is the biggest company in the digital graphics industry. Getting an Adobe certification will go a long way to boost your career. The software you may have to pay attention to include Adobe Photoshop, Adobe Illustrator, Adobe Fireworks, Adobe InDesign and CorelDraw. There are a lot of software out there and more software will still be released. The internet is at your fingertips to provide any information you need to know.

Digital Photography

Digital photography is one of the most exciting careers in the multimedia industry. It is dependent on passion and has a much lower entry requirement compared to video and audio production. Photography is capturing and making a special moment last forever. Photography involves capturing anything in pictures and trying to tell stories with pictures.

However, professional digital photography is more than taking pictures and capturing interesting moments. How well you tell a story with pictures will determine the attention you get in the industry. You can tell good photographers by looking at their pictures. This happens with the help of light, special lenses, and image editing software.

Photography is becoming very fundamental to our human evolution. We are becoming more visual in our decision making. People now make better decisions because of what they can see; this is why most of our devices have a camera.

Business owners understand this, that's why there is a growing demand for professional photography in every sector of the business world.

A career in digital photography means that you have to be very good with a digital camera. You must understand fundamental things about cameras like lenses, focal length, shutter speed, aperture and depth of field, lights, composition, landscapes, frames, layers, background and perspective.

Various types of photography require different skill sets and types of equipment. Some popular photography includes:

1. Industrial Photographers -They take photos for commercial use. These photographers take pictures of objects, models, landscapes, buildings, merchandise, machinery, workers, and other products that companies and businesses use in corporate branding and communications, public relations, advertisement, online media and business strategies. Industrial photographers work with digital graphics designers in the creative department of a company. Fashion photographers fall into this category. They work with a team of makeup artist, stylist, and lighting crew in diverse environment and locations.

2. Event Photographers - They capture pictures at events. These types of photographers can be freelancers. They can also work in a media or public relations company.

3. Photojournalists - They work with any media company capturing news and social happenings. It can be demanding, exciting and sometimes dangerous. Photojournalists are sometimes exposed to danger while capturing wars, natural disasters and riots.

Other types of photography include natural, wildlife, aerial, street, food, sport, portrait, conceptual, architectural, and travels.

Aside from being good with using your camera, knowing how to use photo software is also important. Adobe is the industry leader in this space, understanding their software like Adobe Photoshop, Lightroom in the Adobe Creative suite and getting certified would be great for your career. There are other tons of free photography software, with several more being released. Again, the internet is at your fingertips to provide additional information you need to know.

Digital Film Making and Video Production

The video industry is definitely one of the most complex yet creative areas in the multimedia industry. A career in digital filmmaking and video production can be very rewarding, however, the entry level is much higher and complex than most of the other multimedia career options. Learning digital filmmaking is quite expensive and the equipment required to start your journey in this space isn't cheap. However, the high entry requirements are the same reasons why it is very profitable and rewarding.

Going for a career in digital filmmaking and video production open you up to massive opportunities in various industries. You can work with a movie producer, a television company, news company, advertising and commercials, music videos, events coverage, documentaries and short stories, educational institution and lots more. There are a lot of choices in this career option. They include:

1. Video Production Director
2. Cinematographer
3. Director of Photography
4. Set Designer
5. Movie Editor
6. Visual Effect (VFX)
7. Camera Operator
8. Makeup Artist
9. Screenwriter
10. Costume Designer
11. Music and Sound Engineer
12. Crip
13. Boom Operator
14. Choreographer
15. Crane operator
16. Lighting Technicians

There is so much you can do if you choose a career in digital filmmaking and video production. It takes a lot of hard work, passion, attention to details and commitment to grow in the video industry.

24

Digital Animation

If you are a movie lover like me, you would have watched animation movies like Toy Story, Shrek, and Frozen. These movies are 3D cartoon characters or what is technically called CGI (Computer Generated Images). These types of movies are made with digital animation. Digital animation is one of the most interesting career choices in the multimedia industry. It leverages a lot of human imaginations to bring the impossible to life. Digital animation is not just interesting but also profitable and continues to grow because a huge content of digital animation is targeted at children entertainment and education which is in huge demand.

As a digital animator, you are not limited to creating cartoons for kids; you have a much bigger array of career options in front of you which include:

1.   You can create animated movies like Shrek, Frozen or Toy Story.
2.   You can work with advertising agencies or corporate communications of a huge company to create animated adverts of products for video commercials like doing a TV commercial for a milk product with a cow singing and dancing.
3.   You can work in a video game company. Video game companies need digital animators to create animated characters, environments and games scenes.
4.   You can create educational or school contents. There is no better way for kids

to learn than using animation to get their attention. Digital animators make this happen.

5. Movie productions also use digital animation to create movies like space, action and superhero movies.

6. TV production also needs digital animation to create a montage for starting programmes or special reports and a lot of other production needs.

There are several types of digital animation software you will have to master as you build a career in the animation industry. For beginners, Blender may be a good way to start. It would help you understand the basics of digital animation. However, Autodesk's animation software Maya and 3D Max are the best in the animation industry. They have been used to build some of the world's most wonderful animated movies. There are several other types of software but I would recommend those three.

Career options in the digital animation industry include:

1. Digital Illustrator
2. 2D Computer Animator
3. 3D Computer Animator
4. Stop Motion Animator
5. CG (Computer Generated) Modeller
6. Compositor
7. Digital Painter
8. Layout Artist (2D/3D)
9. Render Wrangler
10. Storyboard Artist

Music Production

Everyone likes good music and technology makes that possible. The music industry is one of the most lucrative industries in the world and technology plays a huge role in the success of the music business.

Music production offers a wide range of career options for those interested. Career options in music production include:

1. Digital Recording Engineer/Mixer
2. Digital Music Producer
3. Disc Jockey (DJ)
4. Studio Manager/Owner
5. Sound Technicians
6. Music Editor
7. Instrument Tech/Specialist
8. Acoustic Consultant
9. Audio Engineer for Videos
10. Digital Remastering Engineer
11. Live Sound Engineer
12. Post-Production Engineer
13. Interactive and Mixed Media Specialist
14. Rerecording Mixer (Film and Video)

Game Development

Many of us played video games while growing up. With the rapid growth of smartphone usage, mobile phones are the gaming device. Mobile devices have played a huge role in the increasing growth of the gaming industry. Digital game development can be tasking, technical and demanding because it brings diverse teams with various skill sets together. Game development involves programming, logic, animation (2D/3D), sounds, and illustration. Despite the diversity of their skill sets, they have to work closely together. Career options for game development include:

1. Game Producer
2. Game Animators
3. Audio Engineer
4. Game Designer
5. Game Programmer
6. Game Artist
7. Level Editor
8. Writer
9. Translator
10. Game Tester

Developing mobile games for starters are relatively easier today with a number of game development engines available online. They are easy to use and do not require much programming. All you need to do is drag and drop your game graphics then set the conditions or logic for their behaviour. There are tons of wonderful game development engine available for free and for sales online.

Some of the most popular game engines for starters include: **GameSalad, Buildbox, Construct 2, Stencyl, Cocos2d-x.**

Advanced game engines for professional game developers include: **Unity, unreal engine, GameMaker Studio 2, Godot Engine, CryEngine, AppGameKit, Amazon Lumberyard, CopperCube 5, RPG Maker, LibGDX.**

Digital Media Content Development and Communication

Increasingly, companies are leveraging on the internet and moving their business operations online. To effectively engage their target audience, companies need to communicate their products and services to their customers through various channels online like social media, blogs, digital adverts, photos and videos. Aside from these media contents, they need to engage with customers who interact with them on these channels. More companies are in need of people equipped with the knowledge and skills to:

1. Handle their online content management function
2. Understand the best ways to target and get the attention of their target audience
3. Effectively address customer feedbacks and responses based on the company's digital activities
4. Select the right set of online channels to help them maximise their online presence
5. Make informed reviews of continuous customer behaviour online
6. Effectively analyse competitors and their digital strategies
7. Constantly keep up to date with the changes in technology

This career path is good for those who are interested in writing, business strategy, copywriting, social media management, digital marketing, online customer care services, public relations, creativity and content development – videos, music, graphic design and music.

Digital Advertising

Several years ago, the only advertising media were newspapers, telephone, flyers, outdoor billboards and radio. Today, we term them traditional advertising. Digital advertising has changed a lot of things in the advertising space. With more than two-thirds of the world's population now online, companies are paying significant attention to digital advertising. More companies are embracing digital marketing because it is cheaper than traditional advertising and you can reach more customers. Aside from the cost and better customer reach, it also allows for interaction between companies and potential customers which you won't get with traditional marketing. Take, for example, a company places an advert in a newspaper and also runs adverts on Instagram for one day. The company will likely get more customers interacting with them on Instagram than through the newspaper. Also, digital marketing provides real-time data to analyse your adverts. This means you can see the exact number of people who clicked on your adverts or viewed it, their gender, age and location. You can't get all these data with traditional advertising. This is why companies today are spending more on digital advertising compared to traditional advertising. The digital advertising industry will continue to grow and companies will need digital advertising professionals to handle online marketing campaigns. According to a recent report by Statista, digital advertising spending would increase from 200.8 billion U.S. dollars in 2015 to 306 billion U.S. dollars in 2020.

The good thing about digital advertising is that it has lower entry requirement. You don't need to learn so much to kick off a career in digital advertising. Your experience on the job is what will make the difference for you. There are a lot of courses online available in this area. It can also be rewarding as you get more experience and you handle bigger advertising campaigns.

In the digital advertising space, Google and Facebook are the kings. You can take the Google digital advertising course online for free and get a certificate to be a Google Certified Digital Advertising Professional. With the knowledge of the Google advertising course, handling adverts on Facebook will be like Christmas holiday.

Customer Service/Help Desk

A critical factor for the growth and success of any company in this digital age is customer service.

How easily can customers reach the company?
What are the customer care channels available to customers?
How quickly can the company attend to customer requests?

Like most other careers, a career in customer service is evolving really fast. The growth in technology is making customers more sophisticated and companies are changing how they handle customer requests and feedbacks. At the centre of the successful customer service is customer satisfaction. Beyond having a call centre, companies are taking advantage of digital tools to create more communication channels between the company and their customers. Aside from phone calls, more companies are offering customer support via direct chats on their website, and using their social media account to promptly address customer needs. Companies are also making use of Customer Relationship Management (CRM) software not just to handle customer requests and feedbacks but also give them unique experiences that make the customer feel special.

A career in customer service has a less technical entry requirement but it requires personality and strength of personal communications. Ability to multi-task and smoothly handle things under quick pressure is also very important in this career option.

By learning how to use CRM software from Zendesk, Microsoft, Saleforce or Zoho, you will be giving yourself the needed advantage to get a customer service job.

Generally, in most tech companies, there are the customer service professionals or help desk specialists who handle general customer inquiry about products and services. There is also the technical customer service professional or help desk technician whose job is more hands-on and technical. They help customers with their devices or solve technical problems via the phone, email, chat or physically in stores.

Data Analysis

One of the biggest benefits of businesses moving online is data generation. Businesses can easily generate data on customers' shopping pattern, purchase history, what they took interest in but did not buy etc. An online e-commerce store can generate data easily and continuously on customers' shopping pattern compared to a physical store which would require more effort and resources. However, generating data is not enough; the question is – What would the company do with the data? The industry has coined a word for this, it is called Big Data. Companies like Facebook, Microsoft, Google and several other tech companies around the world, both big and small, generate a huge amount of data on a daily basis to the tune of terabytes or petabytes.

The beauty of Big Data is not the generation, but it is in the analysis. When companies generate data, they also go a step further to analyse this data to truly understand what the customers really want.

Data analysts process and perform statistical analyses of data; they help businesses translate large figures into plain English to help the business make better decisions. Data analysts scrutinise information using various data analysis tools. They pull out meaningful information from raw data generated by the company to help their employers identify various trends in customer demands and behaviour, pricing structure, marketing matrix and success, analysis of Return on Investment and other analysis-based facts that the business needs to pay attention to. Some of their duties include setting up computerised models to mine or extract meaningful information from big data, assess the quality of the data, filter out invalid data, analyse and interpret results using standard statistical tools and techniques, identify new or emerging opportunities, pinpoint trends, correlations and patterns in complicated data sets, design and maintain data management systems etc.

Skills required to build a career in data analysis include analytical skills, attention to details, passion for math and statistics, communication skills, critical thinking, numerical skills, database management, statistical methodologies and data analysis techniques, ability to produce graphical representations and data visualisations like infographics for presentation. A university degree in statistics, mathematics, computer science, information management or economics would be a good advantage. Job roles under data analysis include data analyst, data scientist, data architect, statistician, data engineer, business/marketing analyst. The demand for professionals in this field is increasing rapidly and it cuts across multiple industries like banking, healthcare, government, sales/marketing, education, finance and investment.

Product Designing

If you run a business, you are doing one of these – selling a product, offering a service or doing both. Whatever the case, how a company designs their product or service delivery is very important to their overall success as a company. Apple is a perfect example of how a company can succeed in producing quality product design to enhance the customer experience while using their products and services.

Apple has remained one of the most valuable companies in the world for some years now. The secret to their continued success is product design. Apple sells products and offers services however one thing remains constant in both areas – the outstanding quality of their designs. From iPhone to iPad to iMac, Mac Book to Apple Watch, their range of products stands out with their product design. Even while using services like iCloud, iTunes, App Store you can see the consistent quality in the designs and the seamless user experience.

Within the realm of product design, there is a number of interesting career options you can explore. They include:

1. Tech Business Strategist

Business Strategists are the ones that ask the really important questions and create a direction for how the company should go with their products and services. They try to understand what customers need or potentially need and create a product or service based on this need. They identify business value based on market and customer research thus bringing up ideas for potential new products and services. They ask questions like, "What should we do next"? "Why should we do it"? "Why are we doing this"? "Is there a market for this product or service we are planning to build"? They analyse the business side and market value of new ideas before the company decides to invest money in building the product or providing the service.

2. Prototypers

After the company has agreed to proceed with the development of a new product or service, Prototypers get to work. They transform the mental pictures into reality. They produce the first physical draft of the product or service. For physical products, it could be sketches on paper, 3D model of the product on a computer, 3D printing of the product prototype. For services, it could diagrams and flowcharts to develop how the service should function. Prototypers bring to reality the idea. They help the company test ideas quickly and cheaply. Prototypes are like the structural frame of the actual thing.

3. User Experience Designers – UX Designers

Prototypers usually work in this department. UX Design focuses on how a product should look or how a service should run. Their primary focus is to create a product or service that is really easy to use and gives users the best experiences. They study user behavioural patterns and explore usability ideas that are targeted toward how the product or service can easily solve the pre-identified need of a user. User experience design is a continuous process, they keep making iterations aimed at enhancing usability and pleasure customers derive from using the product or service thus improving customer satisfaction and loyalty. UX Designers put the mould on the frame the prototypers build.

4. User Interface Designers – UI Designers

User interface designers bring in the whistles and the bells. They are the graphics/visual designers. Once the prototyping and user experience design are done, UI Designers fire up their graphic design software and get down to work. The beautifully designed layouts, icons, images, buttons and colours you see on products, websites and mobile apps are the creative works of the UI Designers. They add the colour, beauty and elegance to the final product design. While UX Designers focus on how to create a journey for customers to solve their products using the product, UI Designers focus on the final looks and feel of the product. UI Designers add the final whistles and bells (colours, pictures, text and layout) to the mould.

For tech products and services, after the product designs, the product developers (software developers/programmers) take over to make the product functional.

Computer Programming and Software Development

Software and computer programming is what the tech industry revolves around. At the foundation of the tech industry are complex computer networks and massive software that run across these networks. The only language a computer understands, as complex as it may seem, is binary - series of ZEROS and ONES. Everything you see on the computer - text, images, colours, videos and audios are all series of ZEROS and ONES to the computer. Unfortunately, binary numbering is too complex for the human mind to process easily. This is why we have the software. It acts as the bridge between human and computers interaction. A software, which is usually in human language, helps us to carry out specific tasks on the computer by translating our intended actions to the computer in binary form, when the computer responses to our request, the software translates the computer's binary feedback to us in human language. Therefore, for computers to do what we want, we have to program them by developing software.

Computer programmers write and test codes that allow computer applications, software programs and computer operating system to function properly. These codes turn computer programs created by software developers into a set of instructions a computer can follow. To build a successful career in computer programming and software development, it is advisable to get a university degree in computer science, mathematics, information systems or any related field. While getting a degree is not a prerequisite to being successful programmers, four years in school studying computers in school will go a very long way to broaden your understanding and give you a deeper understanding of the concepts of computing. This will make you a rock solid programmer. With tons of computer programming and software development lessons online, you can teach yourself computer programming and be outstanding at it. This career path is quite complex and one of the most technical career choices in the tech industry; interestingly it is also one of the most rewarding. Computer programmers and software developers are some of the most well-paid tech professionals across the world and there is an increased demand for them. Being a programmer or a software developer requires passion, patience, critical thinking, problem-solving, attention to details, troubleshooting and a lifetime of continuous learning.

To develop software, you have to learn some computer programming language. Most professionals in this field learn and become proficient with multiple programming languages. Depending on the nature of their work, an average software developer learns about six programming languages but there are three languages they are really good at. For starter, it is better to start with focusing on one language, become proficient in it before you decide to explore others. The choice of programming language to learn depends largely on the work you do, each programming language has its strength and weakness.

There are more than 80 computer programming languages, but for this book, I will focus on a list of top programming languages that are in high demand in the tech industry as of the year 2017 and what they are best used for.

Most recent programming languages are used to create software for these four areas:

1. **Computer Based Software** – It is a software you download and install on your computers before you can use them. Microsoft Office is an example of this.

2. **Web-Based Software (Web Apps)** – It is software that runs on any web browser, no installation is required on your computer. All you need is the internet or a local network to access a certain address through your computer's browser. Facebook, Twitter, Gmail, Amazon, Yahoo are examples of web-based software. To successfully be a web programmer or web developer, it is important to know HTML and CSS.

3. **Mobile Software (Mobile Apps)** – It is the latest type of software for mobile devices. This software runs on mobile device operating systems like iOS, Android or Windows Mobile. WhatsApp, Instagram Mobile App, Snapchat are all examples of mobile software.

4. **Hardware Controls** – It is a type of software used to program computer hardware. These are used for robotics, smart devices like alarms, locks, motion detectors and so on. Internet of Things (IoT) is beginning to look like one of the next big things for the tech industry and would leverage hardware controls heavily. IoT aims to make every device smarter and connected to the internet. For example for a smart home, you can control almost every part of the house with a smartphone. You can be at work and can control almost any device in your house via your mobile phone.

Top programming languages needed by companies around the world in recent times are:

Programming Language	Description	Strengths
Java	Java was developed in the 1990s by Sun Microsystem. It has remained one of the most versatile programming languages to date. It is used for major enterprise software and hardware, web, games, and mobile apps. Android native apps are currently built with Java. Java is designed so robustly that it can work across multiple platforms.	Computer Web Mobile Hardware
Python	Python is a general-purpose programming language. It is used for building websites, web-based and computer-based software and mobile apps. It is popular because it is considered a fairly easy programming language for beginners to start with. Presently, it has a high demand in the tech industry, especially for web-based software.	Computer Web Mobile
PHP	PHP (Hypertext Processor) is a server-side scripting language. It is designed to build websites and web-based software. PHP is the most popular server-side language for developing web apps. Currently, it powers more than 60% of the web and it is still growing. It is easy for beginners and can do a lot when combined with JavaScript and SQL. PHP is one of the languages used to build Facebook and Yahoo. WordPress, Joomla, drupal the popular blogging and CMS platforms are built with PHP.	Web
C#	C#, pronounced as C-Sharp, is a programming language. It combines various aspects of C and C++. It was developed by Microsoft for their .NET software framework and used majorly to build software for Microsoft and Windows platforms. It is popular among developers that create software for Microsoft platforms. C# is used to build ASP (Microsoft's version of PHP) web software.	Computer Web Mobile

C++	C++ is built out of C. It is used in high-performance software and large-scale software infrastructure. It is a powerful programming language still used to build computer software, system software, gaming engines and web-based applications. Most of Microsoft products, Firefox browser, and Adobe products like Photoshop and Adobe reader are built with C++. It is not easy to learn for beginners but the demand for C++ programmers is huge and can be very rewarding.	Computer Hardware
C	C is one of the oldest programming languages still in use today. It is considered the grandfather of all programming languages. Created in the 1970s, C is still widely used in the tech industry as a core programming language. It inspired the creation of popular languages like Java, C#, Python. It is used for operating systems, embedded applications, hardware programming and network devices. It is not so easy to learn but knowing how to program with it is rewarding because there is a good demand for C programmers.	Computer Hardware
Objective-C	Objective-C is another programming language built out of C. It is an object-oriented programming language used by Apple for their operating systems. This language is used to build Apple's OS X and iOS. It remains in high demand because it can be used to create iPhone apps. With Apple launching a new programming language called Swift which aims to be simpler, modern and friendlier for beginners, the demand for Objective-C to create iPhone apps might just be waning as more businesses make a switch to Swift for their iPhone app development.	Computer Mobile

Swift	Swift is one of the most recent programming languages developed by Apple and introduced to developers in 2014. It is a general-purpose language built for Apple's line of operating systems which include iOS, macOS, watchOS, tvOS and Linux. For programmers who intend to build software or apps on Apple's line of products, Swift is the way to go. It allows you to build apps across Apple's multiple devices and platform - phone, TV, laptop, watch and tablet. For beginners, I would recommend learning Swift over Objective-C for your iOS developments.	Mobile Computer
Ruby	Ruby is a general-purpose, object-oriented scripting language for building websites, web-based software and mobile apps. Ruby is powered by the "Ruby on Rails" framework. It is friendly for beginners. Shopify, Airbnb, Slideshare and more were built with Ruby on Rails.	Web Mobile
JavaScript	JavaScript is the most popular scripting language. It is used in conjunction with other server-side scripting languages like PHP to develop websites and web apps. It is not related to Java programming language. It is a client-side scripting language used for front-end web and mobile development. Most web browsers have JavaScript interpreters embedded in so it is compatible across all browsers. JavaScript libraries and front-end frameworks like jQuery, React, Bootstrap, AngularJS, Vue, and Ember are more popular among web developers across the world. In recent times, JavaScript is evolving because of its compatibility and wide usage for web and mobile apps. Using Node.js, JavaScript can be used as a server-side scripting language. Using jQuery Mobile, React Native, PhoneGap and so on, you can build mobile apps from JavaScript. There is a promising future ahead for JavaScript. I would recommend beginners to learn or keep an eye on JavaScript.	Web Mobile

Kotlin	It is the official alternative programming language to Java for building Android Apps. Kotlin is a statically-typed programming language that runs on the Java virtual machine. It can be compiled to JavaScript source code or use the LLVM compiler infrastructure. It is simpler to learn and use compared to Java. It runs faster than Java. Kotlin became popular after Google announced its official decision to make it the third official android programming language aside Java and C++ in May 2017. The demand for Kotlin will likely increase in the coming years.	Web Mobile
R	R is a programming language for mathematicians, statisticians and data analysis. R provides a wide variety of statistical (linear and nonlinear modelling, classical statistical tests, time-series analysis, classification, clustering) and graphical techniques, and is highly extensible. As companies generate data, there is also a need to analyse the data. R is a good language for that.	Computer
SQL	SQL - Structured Query Language is not really a programming language but a language to communicate with and manipulate relational database management systems (RDMS). It cannot solely be used to build software but it is a special language for managing data in databases for software. It is usually combined with all programming language to store and retrieve information from the database. Programming languages cannot directly interact with the database to store and retrieve information. They depend on "SQL queries" to get information from the database and to store information for future use. SQL is a language every programmer should know. It is easy to learn and used by Database administrators. Oracle, MySQL, MSSql all use SQL.	Database

Other languages to note include Go programming Language developed by Google, Perl Programming Language developed by a NASA engineer, Matlab Programming Language similar to R and is used for Data analysis by scientists and the academic environment. For those interested in creating web-based software, it is very important to note that you have to learn and understand how to use HTML, CSS and JavaScript. Although you may not need to major on them, it makes you a better web developer. More on web development, HTML, CSS and JavaScript are in the web design/development section of the book.

Mobile App Development

Mobile devices are getting more powerful, so also are the things we can do on them. Mobile apps continue to expand the possibilities of what we can do with our mobile devices. As mobile phones give more people easy and quick access to the internet, the demand for mobile apps will continue

to grow. Android and iOS are the leading mobile operating systems with Android being the most popular and Windows Mobile being the least popular. Android is built and managed by Google; it is used by major smartphone manufacturers like Samsung, Huawei, LG, Motorola, Xiaomi, Lenovo, Asus, HTC and so many others. iOS is an Apple product that powers the iPhone and iPad. Windows Mobile is made by Microsoft for their phones and tablets. These three mobile operating systems use three very different programming languages for their app development. Android uses Java and recently a programming language called Kotlin, iOS uses Objective-C and Swift, while Windows Mobile uses C#. Learning the three may be a challenge so you may have to determine which one you prefer.

In terms of mobile app development, there are three types of mobile apps:
1. Native Mobile Apps
2. Web Apps
3. Progressive Web Apps

Native Mobile Apps: These are apps built using the original programming languages of the mobile operating system: Swift or Objective-C for iOS apps, Java for Android Apps and C# for Windows apps. Native Apps are the best type of apps because the app is faster for users; it integrates better with the mobile device and is easily distributed on the various app stores (Google Play Store, Apple's App Store and Windows Store). However, these types of app are expensive to develop because it can only work on the mobile operating system it was built for, thus companies have to spend extra money to develop another version that works for the other platforms. So if you intend to build an Android and iOS apps for a business idea, you have to hire and pay two separate teams. Users would have to download and install these types of apps from Google Play, Apple App or Windows Store.

Web Mobile Apps: These are apps built with HTML, CSS and JavaScript. They run on the mobile device browser like a regular website. All smartphones have web browsers, and to use this type of app, you simply access it via a web browser. There is no need to download apps from an app store to your mobile device. A web app can work for any mobile operating system as long as the device has a browser. It is easier to build and maintain for companies however it is much slower than native mobile apps. It is also not as interactive and its features are not as extensive as what you get with a native mobile app.

Progressive Web Apps: These type of apps try to integrate both native and web app features. Usually built with HTML, CSS and JavaScript and placed in a native mobile app structure. Through the use of APIs (Application programming interface), it accesses some of the features of native apps. Therefore, rather than creating two versions of a mobile app for iOS and Android, mobile app programmers can create one app and fit it into iOS and Android native app structure. This offers a cheaper way for companies to build and maintain mobile apps. However, its functionalities are still not as extensive as the native mobile app and there is no need to download the app, it uses your device browser so for now the apps like this can not be uploaded to Google Play or Apple App store.

Generally, if you are thinking of a career in Mobile App development, you have to like any of the other dominant mobile operating system to learn. Generally, building iOS app can be more rewarding than Android because Apple devices are used by the richest customers around the world who pay well for good services, unlike Android that has a mass market. Apple is also very strict with approving apps on their App Store so you have to learn a lot about Apple's App standards before developing your iOS Apps. For Android, it is relatively easier to develop and get your apps approved.

Database Administration

Data storage and management remain one of the most critical aspects of the IT industry. While software may be the heart of the IT world, data is the blood that flows through its veins. Without data, software is simply chunks of computer code doing nothing. All software requires some form of data to perform its task optimally; therefore data storage and management are central to all business at this age.

A database is an organised collection of data, while Database Management System (DBMS) is software specifically built to interact with users and other software to capture, store and analyse data. Database administrators (fondly called DBAs) are the tech professionals in charge of all functions involved in database development, performance, storage, security and retrieval. They work with database management systems software and determine ways to organise, store and secure data.

As more businesses increase their dependence on technology for their business operations, the need for database administrators is growing.

To get started in this field, it is important to learn SQL - Structured Query Language which is used to manage most of the popular database Management System used by big businesses. Popular DBMSs include MySQL, PostgreSQL, EnterpriseDB, MongoDB, MariaDB, Microsoft SQL Server, Oracle, Sybase, SAP HANA, MemSQL, SQLite and IBM DB2. Oracle remains the leader in this industry and is used for some of the largest tech projects in the world. Microsoft SQL Server is also very popular for large-scale projects while for MySQL which is the free and open source is popular for general use. Right now, there is a huge demand for professionals who are proficient in Oracle, Microsoft SQL Server, IBM DB2 and MySQL.

There are three major professional certifications for database administration:

- Oracle Database Certification
- Microsoft Certified Solutions Expert (MCSE) – Data Platform or Business Intelligence
- IBM Certified Database Administrator

Being a certified database administrator is a step away from getting well-paying jobs.

Computer Support and System Administration

Computers and computer networks are very important assets to most companies today. When there is an issue with a computer, server or network within the office and it is not promptly fixed, this can have a serious impact on the business operation. This translates into a financial loss for the company. For staff within the company having technical issues with their computers or accessing the company network, the computer support and system administrator is usually the first point of call.

System administrators review technical issues, gather information from users, troubleshoot system hardware and software to define and fix the problem. Sometimes, they work directly with software and hardware vendors to set up new solutions or to fix an existing problem. For more difficult issues, they have to do a lot of research, go through several documentations while troubleshooting a technical problem so they can pinpoint the solution to specific network problems.

A system administrator ensures the right people have access to the right computers and accounts; makes sure internet services are constantly available to all users within the company; carry out routine software and hardware maintenance to ensure optimal performance; replace damaged computer hardware and analyse system logs to see any potential issues with the computer. This job requires a vast understanding of computer hardware, software and network systems. Professional certification will always give you an edge. Some of the certifications available to make you a Professional System Administrator are Microsoft Certified Solutions Expert (MCSE), Cloud Platform and Infrastructure, CompTIA Server+, Red Hat Certified Engineer (RHCE), and Oracle Linux System Administrator.

Web Design and Development

In the world of web design and development, HTML is king. You cannot do web design and development without HTML.

Hypertext Markup Language (HTML) is the standard markup language for creating web pages and web applications. It is not a programming language. It is a frontend language used to instruct the browser on what to display. To be a web programmer, you surely have to know HTML which is why is it important to mention it at this point.

Cascading Style Sheets (CSS) is a style sheet language used for describing the presentation of a document written in a markup language.

HTML and CSS are combined with JavaScript to build the outlook (client-side) of websites and web apps that we see and interact with.

HTML5, CSS 3 and JavaScript are the latest technology used for client-side scripting. It is very important to understand how to use these three along with a server-side language like PHP, Ruby, ASP or Python for you to be proficient in web programming or web app development. HTML and CSS are very easy to learn, and most beginners do not find them difficult.

There is a big difference between web design and web development, but first, let's explore how the internet works.

The internet simply has two major sides —client side and the server side. As a regular

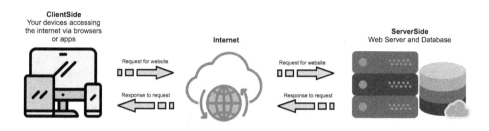

user browsing the internet, what you see is the client side of the internet – the beautiful images, videos, colours and text you see on web pages. However, the server side is what really controls what you see on the client side. It hosts the database and programming scripts that process your client-side requests. For example, you want to login to your Gmail account, when you type **www.gmail.com** and submit, your request is sent to the server side of Google which first checks if you are logged in already or not. If you are not logged in, the server side sends back a login page to you on the client side to log in. Once you enter your username and password and submit, it is securely sent to the server side to first validate your login details if it is correct or not; if it is correct the server side ensures that out of the pool of billions of email messages on the Google servers, you only see the ones meant for you on the client side. That's how the internet simply works. At the client side of the internet, we have HTML which handles how web pages are displayed in browsers, CSS which handles styling of web pages and JavaScript adds dynamic effects to web pages. On the server side, we have the web server which hosts the software that helps to interpret programming scripts for PHP, ASP, Ruby, Python or Java. Aside from this, it also hosts the database where information is stored. The server is configured to interpret client-side request based on the scripts on it and also to interface with the database to revert information which will be sent back to client-side users.

Therefore, the difference between web design and development is this – web designers are not programmers, they are digital graphics designers with knowledge of HTML and CSS, their primary job is to design beautiful web pages which you see on the client side while you are browsing. Web developers are the programmers; they deal more with the server side of the internet. They are the ones who write the scripts and codes that make web pages designed by web designers function and carry out a task for you.

Back to our Gmail login, the login box you see is designed by a team of web designers using HTML, CSS and JavaScript. The web developers are the ones who write the codes to ensure that when you enter your login details and submit, you can see your emails.

If you are interested in digital graphics and the web, web design is the way you should go. Knowledge of Adobe software is recommended. This includes Adobe Dreamweaver, Photoshop, Illustrator, XD and Muse.

If you have less interest in designs but more interest in programming, web development is the way to go. You will need to learn any of these languages JavaScript, PHP, Ruby, ASP, Python or Java extensively. Aside from the languages, you will need to learn SQL to manage the database. SQL is an integral part of these web-based programming languages.

Currently, JavaScript is getting more attention from the global web development community. JavaScript has always been a client-side scripting language but with the emergence of Node.JS – an open source, cross-platform JavaScript run-time environment for executing JavaScript code server side, JavaScript is increasingly playing a role at the server side. For newcomers in this field, you should pay attention to Node.JS; the demand for Node.JS developers will likely increase in the coming years.

The demand for web designers and developments are on a steady rise and would continue to be for a long time to come. One of the good things about the web design and development skill set is that you can utilise them to build mobile hybrid apps, as such you are not just limited to the web. With further learning, you can easily make use of your skills to develop both Android and iOS apps.

Cyber Security

With companies around the world spending billions of dollars to build online assets and businesses, there is no better time to be a cyber security professional than now. With this trend, the need for adequate security for online assets is very essential. Cyber security professionals are among the most sought-after professionals in the technology industry, with demand for workers in this area outpacing other IT jobs by a wide margin. Presently, with the growing rate of cyber-attacks and malicious intrusion in online networks, cyber security professionals are in very high demand and right now, there is a shortage of good professionals. All industries need cyber security professionals. From 2007 to 2013, the search by corporate organisations for cyber security professionals grew by 73% which is twice faster than any other ICT related job opportunity.

A career in cyber security is diverse, the options include:

1. Chief Information Officer
2. Security Administrator
3. Security Analyst
4. Security Architect
5. Cryptographer
6. Cyber Forensics Expert
7. Cyber Security Specialist
8. Incident Responder
9. Systems Penetration Tester
10. Security Auditor
11. Security Consultant
12. Vulnerability Assessor
13. Security Software Developer

Because of the importance and sensitive role of cyber security, professional certification is essential to get a good job. Cyber security certifications come in all areas which range from forensics, intrusion to ethical hacking. There are independent accrediting organisations like CompTIA, EC Council, GIAC, ISACA and (ISC)2 that offer professional certifications trusted by companies around the world. For starters, you can commence your certification with **CompTIA Security+, GSEC: GIAC Security Essentials Certification, SSCP: Systems Security Certified Practitioner.**

Computer Aided Design (CAD)

Do you have the passion to study engineering, construction or be an inventor and are thinking of how to use technology to design structures or make new inventions? Computer Aided Design, CAD, is what you need.

CAD is used by architects, engineers, drafters, artists, and others to create precision drawings or technical illustrations. CAD software can be used to create two-dimensional (2-D) drawings or three-dimensional (3-D) models. CAD is used extensively in number of industries including construction, civil engineering, architecture, cars and automobile, factory and plant design, mechanical engineering, industrial design, landscape architecture, manufacturing process planning, environmental mapping and surveying, electrical designs and engineering, heating, ventilation and air conditioning, biomechanical systems, water systems, and transportation engineering.

Aside all these, CAD also plays a major role in 3D printing, which is revolutionising how objects are being created. Today, thanks to 3D printing I can sit on my computer, build objects I want using my CAD software and print out that exact object. 3D printing is still emerging and would transform construction, manufacturing and product development in the coming years.

As a CAD expert, you can work in these industries:

- · Architecture
- · Engineering
- · Fashion Design
- · Interior and Exterior Design
- · Game Design
- · Industrial Design
- · Prototyping

Autodesk is the leading company in the CAD industry and has a wide range of CAD software for the industry you are working in. These include AutoCAD, AutoCAD Architecture, AutoCAD Civil 3D, AutoCAD Electrical, AutoCAD Map 3D, 3ds Max, Maya, Revit.

Computer Networking

Computer networking is one of the most diverse fields in the tech industry. There is a continuous increase in the demand for more and better internet service across the world. Tech companies are always innovating and redesigning computer networks to meet this growing demand, therefore computer networks are getting more complex. Computer networks have become the communications backbone of large and small businesses.

Computer network engineers are also called network architects or network administrators. Their job is to plan and construct data communication networks such as Local Area Network (LAN), Wide Area Network (WAN) systems and VPNs (Virtual Private Networks). They are responsible for analysing, designing, installing and configuring computer networks for companies. They monitor network performance, maintain network security, troubleshoot and solve network problems.

Analytical and problem-solving skills are some of the greatest gifts a successful network engineer should have -the ability to solve problems quickly and creatively. A vast knowledge of computer hardware, network software and network devices like cables, routers, switches, and firewalls is very essential. It is also important to note that computer networking, unlike other tech fields, involves a lot of physical activities handling various computer hardware and network devices.

Some of the job roles in this career path include:

- · Network Administrator
- · Network Engineer
- · Network Technician
- · Network Programmer/Analyst
- · Network/Information Systems Manager
- · Network Security

A university degree in computer science, information systems, electrical electronics or any related field would be a good place to start. Professional certifications are also very essential for this field. In the world of computer networking, CISCO is king so you can kick off your certifications with Cisco certifications – there is a huge demand for Cisco certified professionals. Microsoft, Juniper, Nortel, Sun Microsystems, CompTIA and Novell all have network professional certification programs. The demand for computer network professionals would continue to grow. Professional experience is also a big factor in this field; therefore, while you are studying for your degree or professional certifications, seek opportunities to work somewhere to build practical experience in this field.

IT Project Management

Projects are a big part of the tech industry. Tech teams would always have projects to deliver such as animated videos, promotional photo shoots or designs, new games, mobile apps, and software development. For these projects to be successful there is  a need for a project manager. Every technical team in a tech company needs a project manager to manage the successful delivery of projects. The role of IT project management is less of technical skills and more of administrative and managerial skills.

IT project managers oversee and manage the activities of IT projects. This includes overseeing budgets, managing personnel and schedules, and executing a project communication plan. IT project managers are vital because they supervise all aspects of IT projects and coordinate the technical team to ensure work flows smoothly from start to finish. Their primary goal is to ensure the delivery of a successful project within the scheduled timeframe and allocated budget.

For those interested in the tech industry but not so passionate about developing the core technical skills, this is one of the few career options available to you. It will require you to develop your management, leadership and interpersonal relationship skills. The beauty of IT project management is that this professional skill set can be used in any other industry. Project management cuts across multiple industries. A project management certification such as the Project Management Professional (PMP) certification from the Project Management Institute (PMI) is required to validate your expertise and experience. CompTIA Project+ is also another project management certification you can take. However, PMI certified Professionals are in high demand across the world.

Artificial Intelligence and Robotics

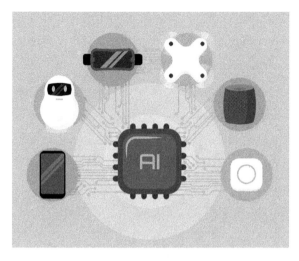

Artificial intelligence and robotics are no doubt one of the fastest growing areas of the tech industry. Machine learning and automation is rapidly growing and getting a lot of attention. Robots have always been with us especially in manufacturing to carry out tasks faster. However, artificial intelligence is a drive towards giving robots their own consciousness and intelligence. No doubt, this field is one of the most controversial of the various IT fields. While it holds a lot of promise and can help solve some of the world's biggest problems, there are concerns about its negative impact in the wrong hands.

Irrespective of how we feel about it, one thing is clear, AI is breaking new grounds and ushering humanity into a new era. Today, we can see the impact of AI on transportation with driverless cars, automated navigations, language translation, national infrastructure management, healthcare, home automation, disaster management and rescue, and hospitality. This field is still emerging and there is a lot of promise ahead of it. A number of universities already offer courses in this field, and there are tons of online materials to help you learn more about it.

Geographical Information Systems

Maps and navigation systems are increasingly becoming an integral part of the on-going revolution in the tech industry. Mapping and automated navigation systems are made possible because of Geographical Information Systems (GIS). The use of GIS goes far beyond maps and navigation system. It is used in diverse fields like environment planning, rural/urban development, wildlife management, health care delivery, security analysis, transportation, conflict resolution, business planning and marketing, human migration and population control, weather and climate change, agricultural planning etc.

Geographic information systems (GIS) specialists work with a large database containing geological and spatial information such as satellite images and aerial photographs. This information is used to make maps, develop specialised software, or analyse data for scientific, commercial or planning purposes.

Job roles of GIS specialists include maps creation, collection of geographical information, digitising physical maps and combining them with other data sets, storage of geographical information, analysis and presentation of geographical information, the compilation of geographic and demographic data from various sources, analysing and modelling of relationships between geographic data sets. Automated transportation is one of the latest and fastest growing fields in the tech industry. Its success would not only depend on artificial intelligence, it will also heavily rely on GIS. As technology opens up possibilities for more industries, the need for GIS specialists will continue to grow.

Telecom Engineering

It is safe to say that telecom engineers are the true creators of the internet. They build the internet's backbone that runs across the world. Telecommunications engineers provide services and engineering solutions revolving around different modes of communication and information transfer such as wireless telephony services, radio and satellite communications, internet and broadband technologies, fibre optic cabling, complex networks and switching systems.

The role of a telecoms engineer is to design and oversee the installation of telecommunications equipment and facilities such as complex electronic switching systems, and other plain old telephone service facilities, optical fibre cabling, IP networks, and microwave transmission systems. The continuous growth and expansion of internet access largely depend on telecoms engineering. Recent statistics show that about 49% of the world population is yet to be connected to the internet; therefore there are a lot of opportunities ahead for aspiring telecoms engineers. Aside from internet growth and expansion, current internet services are also being upgraded to be faster and smarter. The rise of the Internet of Things, automation and artificial intelligence is giving us reasons to upgrade our current internet infrastructure across the world.

This career path will require a university degree in electrical electronics, telecoms engineering, physics or any other related course.

For Tech trainings,videos and resources

Visit : www.iamadedoyin.com

Join or follow the conversation with the hashtag

#BeTechPro

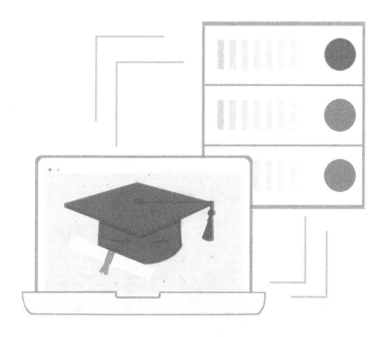

SECTION 4

PROFESSIONAL ICT CERTIFICATIONS

ICT certifications put an official seal on your skills as an ICT professional. Taking professional ICT certification courses and getting certified help boost your reputation in the technology industry. Since you are considering a career in ICT, certifications are very important to your career development. Being skilful and knowledgeable in your field of technology is good and would open opportunities for you. Certifications, however, make it easy to land an interview in with some of the big companies.

Two groups of people I have seen over the years in technology:

1. Very skilled tech professionals, usually self-taught, who don't really care about certification. This is good. Certification, however, is the way to go if you intend to build a good career in the technology industry and work in the best companies. Remember, it is your CV and the documents you attach that would first introduce you to employers before they decide to meet you in person. Most big companies have a strict hiring process. You may be good at what you do but if your CV isn't good enough for them to consider you for an interview, you may lose opportunities.

2. Tech professionals that chase certifications. Usually, these are people that aren't passionate about tech, but consider it an industry they can make good money from. They acquire as many certifications as possible to have an impressive CV so they can get a good job. The danger of this is certification may get you through the door but your tech skill set will determine how long you retain the job.

My advice is to settle for a field of technology you are really passionate about, learn and devote yourself to being the best at it, then get certified to put an official seal on your tech skills.

Every aspect of ICT has an industrial leader; for example, Cisco is the industry leader in networking, Adobe is the industry leader in multimedia and Oracle is the industry leader in database systems. These industry leaders have their software and products used by the biggest companies in the world. Therefore, to confirm that you truly understand their software and products, it is important you earn a certificate or badge which you can present along with your CV to companies you intend to work for.

Each of these industry leaders has a certification examination you can take to be officially recognised as a tech professional who understands their software. So let's take a look at these tech industry leaders and their certifications.

Before you sit for any certification examination, you have to search online for an accredited ICT certification test centre in your country. Some test centres offer training or self-study packs which you can use to prepare for the examination. Most of the certification exams aren't free; some are free but occasionally vendors offer promotional discounts which lower the cost.

Adobe

Adobe is the king of multimedia – digital graphics, prints, web, audio, visual effects and video. If your passion is media, your eyes should be on Adobe. Adobe has an extensive range of software applications. There are three levels of Adobe certification:

1. Single Product Certification

This is just to show your expertise in any of the Adobe software. However, I wouldn't advise you to settle for this because it doesn't give your career a focus.

2. Specialist Certification

This certifies you as a specialist in a specific medium: print, web or video. Specialist certification is available for Adobe Creative Cloud or Creative Suite products. I highly recommend this to you as you build your career in media.

Adobe Certified Experts (ACE) must pass the current version of all required (R) exams and an elective (E) within any given certification track.

	Design Specialist	Web Specialist	Video Specialist	Rich Internet App. Specialist	Technical Comm. Specialist	eLearning Suite Specialist
Adobe Photoshop	E	E	R	E		E
Adobe InDesign	R					
Adobe Dreamweaver		R		E		E
Adobe Illustrator	E	E		E		
Adobe Acrobat	R				E	
Adobe Premiere Pro/Encore DVD/OnLocation			R			
Adobe After Effects			E			
Adobe Cold Fusion		E		R		
Adobe Flash		R	E	R		E
Adobe Flex		E		R		
Adobe FrameMaker	E				R	
Adobe RoboHelp					R	
Adobe Captivate					E	R
Adobe Captivate with eLS extensions						R

3. Master Certification

This certification recognises your expertise in the entire Adobe Creative Suite products. It solidifies your professionalism in the creative and multimedia industry.

CS Design Master	CS Web Master	CS Video Master
• Adobe Acrobat Professional • Adobe InDesign • Adobe Illustrator • Adobe Photoshop	• Adobe Acrobat Professional • Adobe Dreamweaver • Adobe Flash • Adobe Illustrator • Adobe Photoshop	• Adobe After Effects • Adobe Flash • Adobe Illustrator • Adobe Photoshop • Adobe Premiere Pro

Autodesk

Autodesk Inc. is a leader in the 2D and 3D Computer Aided Design, engineering and entertainment software industry. Autodesk has some of the best set of 3D software in the world. Their software is used across the manufacturing, architecture, building, construction, product design, construction, media and entertainment industries. Autodesk software is in the centre of the new evolution of 3D building and printing. Autodesk has three levels of certifications for all their software:

Autodesk Certified User

Those who are relatively new to Autodesk software and want to demonstrate basic proficiency can seek to become Certified Users. Certification of this level shows a commitment to academic success or career development.

Autodesk Certified Professional

Those who possess more advanced skills and can solve complex workflow and design challenges should seek recognition as Certified Professionals. Certification of this level shows you have the skills needed to stand out from the competition and pursue career advancement.

Autodesk Certified Specialist

Those who possess a competency in specialised workflow or mastery of an Autodesk Suite can earn a Certified Specialist credential. Certification of this level demonstrates the ability to design innovative solutions across multiple technologies.

Here is the list of Autodesk Software:
- AutoCAD
- Autodesk 3ds Max
- Autodesk AutoCAD Civil 3D
- Autodesk Inventor
- Autodesk Maya
- Autodesk Revit Architecture
- Autodesk Revit MEP
- Autodesk Revit Structure

Cisco

Cisco is the largest networking and computer infrastructure company in the world. It specialises in designing, manufacturing and selling of network equipment to leading companies across the world. If you intend to build a career in computer networking, telecoms or large scale computer infrastructure, Cisco certification is the way to go. Cisco certifications include:

- CCENT - Cisco Certified Entry Networking Technician
- CCNA - Cisco Certified Network Associate
- CCDA - Cisco Certified Design Associate
- CCNP - Cisco Certified Network Professional
- CCDP - Cisco Certified Design Professional
- CCSP - Cisco Certified Security Professional
- CCIE - Cisco Certified Internetwork Expert

As the internet expands and more services depends on internet infrastructure for their operations, the need for Cisco professionals will steadily increase in the coming years.

Certified Internet Web Professional (CIW)

Certified Internet Web Professional (CIW) is the leading vendor-neutral certification series for Information Technology (IT). The CIW core certification focuses on the foundational standards and job skills that enable the internet to function, including web design, development, e-commerce, administration, networking, databases and security. CIW is comprised of an extensive series of curriculum and high stakes certification examinations, teaching IT in foundational and specific career path subject matters.

The CIW Web Foundations Series

This course is the most popular vendor-neutral web education program in the world. It consists of three courses. Individuals who have completed all three CIW Web Foundations Associate courses have mastered more than digital literacy skills. They will have a unique understanding of internet business, data networking and website design. This program transforms internet consumers into producers of internet-based technologies.

The CIW Web and Mobile Design Series

This is ideal for professionals, with some web development knowledge, who work in the fields of website design, e-commerce, mobile applications and graphic design, as well as entrepreneurs who want to be able to develop and manage their businesses online.

The CIW Web Development Series

This includes the essential combination of a front-end scripting language, a back-end programming language and the skills to integrate them with a database. Due to this diversity, individuals who complete these series become valuable corporate IT team member.

The CIW Web Security Series

This course is for those who configure, manage and deploy e-business solutions servers and implement e-business and network security solutions. An individual can obtain three levels of credentials to recognise their proficiency in networking administration and to validate their competence in security.

CompTIA

CompTIA is the voice of the world's information technology (IT) industry. As a non-profit trade association, it advances the global interests of IT professionals and IT channel organisations. It enables them to be more successful with industry-leading IT certifications and IT business credentials, IT education, resources and the ability to connect with like-minded, leading IT industry experts.

CompTIA A+ Certification Training

This is an entry-level certification well respected in the tech industry. CompTIA A+ credentials cover the basics of IT administration, installation, networking, security and support in a widely recognised vendor-neutral qualification.

CompTIA Network+ Certification Training

This certification demonstrates competency in network installation, management and maintenance. This is good if you are planning a career in networking.

CompTIA Linux+ Certification Training

This certifies you as a Linux administrator. Linux is an operating system, like Microsoft Windows, used extensively in various areas of the technology industry.

CompTIA Project+ Certification Training

CompTIA's Project+ is an IT project management certification that is respected. It is easier to pass than the major project management certifications like PMI.

CompTIA Security+ Certification Training

CompTIA Security+ certification covers a broad base of knowledge in security practices and technology. With the growing rate of cyber challenges, security is very important and this certification is a good start.

CompTIA Server+ Certification Training

Server+ certification offers a vendor-neutral certification to show your competency in server administration.

EC-Council

EC-Council

The International Council of Electronic Commerce Consultants (EC-Council) is the leading IT and e-Business certification awarding body and the creator of the world famous Certified Ethical Hacker (CEH), Computer Hacking Forensics Investigator (CHFI) and EC-Council Certified Security Analyst (ECSA)/License Penetration Tester (LPT) programs.

Popular certifications include:

EC-Council CEH Certification - Certified Ethical Hacker

Getting certified as an EC- Council Ethical Hacker provides you with the professional skills needed to be a cyber security specialist. You will understand the best defence against network security breaches, secure data across the network, find and eliminate system vulnerabilities. As computer networks become more advanced, it is the job of the ethical hacker to take pre-emptive measures against malicious attacks.

EC-Council CHFI Certification - Computer Hacking Forensic Investigator

Computer forensics is the application of cyber investigation and analysis techniques across a computer network to acquire potential legal evidence against hackers who carry out malicious cyber-attacks. This legal evidence ranges from misuse of technology, cyber fraud, email scams, stealing or destruction of intellectual property, theft of trade secrets, to the spread of viruses, Trojan horses and other malicious programs.

The EC-Council's Computer Hacking Forensic Investigator certification makes you a professional at detecting hacking attacks, extracting evidence to report the crime and conduct audits to prevent future attacks.

Oracle

Oracle is one of the largest software companies in the world. It has an extensive range of certifications. Oracle's biggest strength is database systems. Oracle is the king of database products for big corporation across the world. Therefore, if you are looking at building a career in database administration, Oracle Certification is the way to go.

Oracle Database technology is used by the world's leading companies to manage critical business functions, systems and processes, with 305,000 top companies trusting their critical systems to Oracle Database. By investing the time to earn **Oracle Database Certifications**, you'll develop the expertise you need to work on the number one database in the world.

Aside database system, Oracle has more than 64 Oracle Applications, Oracle Cloud, Oracle Enterprise Management, Java programming Language, Solaris Operating systems and Virtualisation.

There are different levels of Oracle Certifications. These certifications are spread across 9 technology pillars and further broken down into product family and product groupings. Certifications are also defined by job role on the Oracle Certification website. They are:
- Oracle Certified Associate (OCA)
- Oracle Certified Professional (OCP)
- Oracle Certified Master (OCM)
- Oracle Certified Expert (OCE)
- Oracle Certified Specialist (OCS)

Microsoft

Microsoft is the world's largest software maker by revenue, and one of the world's most valuable companies. Microsoft develops, manufactures, supports and sells computer software, consumer electronics and personal computers and services. Its best-known software products are the Microsoft Windows line of operating systems, Microsoft Office Suite, and the Internet Explorer and Edge web browsers. Its flagship hardware products are the Xbox game consoles and the Microsoft Surface tablet line-up.

Microsoft certification is currently broken into six paths which include :

Mobility
The Mobility competency is designed for those looking to stand out as the expert in powerful, secure mobility management solutions for large businesses.

Cloud: Platform and infrastructure
The Cloud Platform competency is designed for those looking to capitalize on the growing demand for infrastructure and software as a service (SaaS) solutions built on Microsoft Azure.

Productivity
The Cloud Productivity competency is for those looking to deploy Microsoft Office cloud and hybrid solutions to enterprise customers. Differentiate yourself with this competency as a proven cloud solution expert.

Data: Management and Analytics
The Data Management and Analytics competency recognizes those who demonstrate expertise in specific aspects of Microsoft Business Intelligence (BI) solutions to deliver, deploy, and support BI projects.

App Builder
The App Builder competency provides resources to enable faster delivery and continuous improvement in the software delivery organization.

Microsoft

Business Applications

The Business Applications competency recognizes those who demonstrate expertise in specific aspects of Microsoft Dynamics technologies.

Here are some of Microsoft certifications Levels:

- Microsoft Technology Associate (MTA)
- Microsoft Certified Solutions Associate (MCSA)
- Microsoft Certified Solutions Expert (MCSE)
- Microsoft Certified Solutions Developer (MCSD)
- Microsoft Office Specialist (MOS)

Microsoft Certification Path

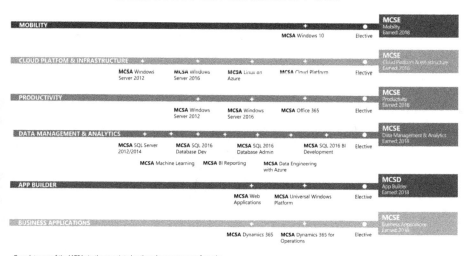

Complete one of the MCSAs in the associated path and pass one exam from the elective exam pool to earn your MCSE or MCSD certification.

Google

Google is generally known as a search engine company. However, Google is more than just a search engine company. It is one of the largest technology companies in the world specialising in internet related services and products. These include online advertising technologies, search engine, cloud computing, and software. Google offer certifications for those interested in a career in digital marketing, e-Commerce, or online collaborations.

Here are Google certifications:

Google AdWords Certification

Google Adwords is the largest online advertising platform in the world. The AdWords exams cover basic and advanced advertising concepts, including campaign set up, management, and optimisation. To become AdWords certified, you'll need to pass the AdWords Fundamentals exam and an additional product area assessment. You can demonstrate your expertise and help your company earn the Google Partner badge with AdWords certification.

Assessment areas are:

- · Ad Words Fundamentals
- · Search Advertising
- · Display Advertising
- · Video Advertising
- · Shopping Advertising
- · Mobile Advertising

Google Analytics Certification

Google Analytics is a free web analytics service that tracks, analyses browsing pattern of website users and reports website traffic. It provides the insights and data needed to make intelligent marketing and business decisions. The Google Analytics Individual

Qualification exam covers basic and advanced Google Analytics concepts. This includes topics such as 1) planning and principles, 2) implementation and data collection, 3) configuration and administration, 4) conversion and attribution, 5) reports, metrics, and dimensions.

· Digital Analytics Fundamentals

· Google Analytics Platform Principles

· e-Commerce Analytics

· Mobile App Analytics Fundamentals

Other Google certifications are **Google for Education Certification** for educators who want to integrate Google apps into education and **Google App Administrator Certification** for administrators who demonstrate the skills required to manage a Google Apps domain.

Project Management

In recent times, the demand for certified project managers has increased not just in the ICT industry but across all major industries around the world. Getting a project management certificate allows you to work in various industries as a project manager. Project Management Institute (PMI) certification is internationally recognised and can be used to work in just about any industry in the world. PMI professional certification ensures that you're ready to meet the demands of projects and employers across the globe.

Here are PMI certifications:

- Project Management Professional (PMP)
- Program Management Professional (PgMP)
- Portfolio Management Professional (PfMP)
- Certified Associate Project Management (CAPM)
- PMI Professional in Business Analysis (PMI-PBA)
- PMI Agile Certified Practitioner (PMI-ACP)
- PMI Risk Management Professional (PMI-RMP)
- PMI Scheduling Professional (PMI-SP)

Amazon Web Services (AWS)

Amazon offers a range of certification including Associate, Professional, and Specialty. The certifications focus on gaining technical knowledge of the Amazon Web Services (AWS) platform. They offer associate certifications covering the roles of Solutions Architect, Developer, and SysOps Administrator. Once you have completed an Associate Certification in any of these roles, you may progress to a Specialty in Advanced Networking or Big Data, or a professional certification in Solutions Architect or DevOps Engineering. Speciality certifications offer advancement for someone interested in validating their expertise in a specific area. Professional certifications are the highest role-specific certification.

ITIL - IT Service Management

ITIL is the most widely accepted approach to IT service management in the world. ITIL can help individuals and organisations use IT to realise business change, transformation and growth.

The ITIL certification scheme provides a modular approach to the ITIL framework and is comprised of a series of qualifications focused on different aspects of ITIL best practice to various degrees of depth and detail.

The tiered structure of the qualification offers candidates flexibility relating to the different disciplines and areas of ITIL and the ability to focus their studies on key areas of interest.
There are five certification levels within the scheme:

Foundation Level

The Foundation level is the entry-level certification which offers you a general awareness of the key elements, concepts and terminologies used in the ITIL service lifecycle, including the links between lifecycle stages, the processes used and their contribution to service management practices.

Practitioner Level

The Practitioner level is the next stage in the ITIL scheme. It has been developed to provide a step between Foundation and the Intermediate level and aims to improve the ability of individuals to adopt and adapt ITIL in their organisations.

Intermediate Level

The Intermediate level certification has a modular structure with each module providing a different focus on IT Service Management. You can take as few or as many Intermediate qualifications as you need. The Intermediate level goes into more detail than the Foundation and Practitioner levels and provides an industry-recognised qualification.

Expert Level

The ITIL Expert level qualification is aimed at those who are interested in demonstrating knowledge of the ITIL Scheme in its entirety. The certificate is awarded to candidates who have achieved a range of ITIL certifications and have attained a well rounded, superior knowledge and skills base in ITIL best practices.

Master Level

To achieve the ITIL Master certification, you must be able to explain and justify how you have personally selected and applied a range of knowledge, principles, methods and techniques from ITIL and supporting management techniques, to achieve desired business outcomes in one or more practical assignments.

(ISC)² Information Security Certifications

The International Information System Security Certification Consortium, or (ISC)², is a non-profit organisation which specialises in training and certifications for cyber security professionals.

- CISSP - Certified Information Systems Security Professional
- SSCP - Systems Security Certified Practitioner
- CCSP - Certified Cloud Security Professional
- CAP - Certified Authorization Professional
- CSSLP - Certified Secure Software Lifecycle Professional
- HCISPP - HealthCare Information Security and Privacy Practitioner
- CISSP-ISSAP - Information Systems Security Architecture Professional
- CISSP-ISSEP - Information Systems Security Engineering Professional
- CISSP-ISSMP - Information Systems Security Management Professional
- Associate of (ISC)2

ISACA Certification

An ISACA certification is an opportunity to enhance your professional credibility. A CISA, CISM, CGEIT or CRISC after your name confirms to employers that you possess the experience and knowledge to meet the challenges of the modern enterprise.

ISACA offers the following certifications:

Certified Information Systems Auditor (CISA)
The CISA certification is world-renowned as the standard of achievement for those who audit, control, monitor and assess an organisation's information technology and business systems.

Certified in Risk and Information Systems Control (CRISC)
CRISC is the only certification that positions IT professionals for future career growth by linking IT risk management to enterprise risk management and positioning them to become strategic partners to the business.

Certified Information Security Manager (CISM)

The management-focused CISM is the globally accepted standard for individuals who design, build and manage enterprise information security programs. CISM is the leading credential for information security managers.

Certified in the Governance of Enterprise IT (CGEIT)

CGEIT recognises a range of professionals for their knowledge and application of enterprise IT governance principles and practices. CGEIT provides you with the credibility to discuss critical issues around governance and strategic alignment based on your recognised skills, knowledge and business experience.

Cyber Security Nexus – CSX Certificate and CSX-P Certification

As the cyber landscape continues to rapidly evolve, it's not enough to rely solely on knowledge and theory. A performance-based CSX certification is a testament to your real-life skills and experience and proclaims that your commitment, tenacity, and abilities exceed expectations. CSX programs and certifications help individuals demonstrate their skills and prove that they know the most current cyber security standards, and offer employers confidence that their employees are up to the demanding tasks.

There are many ICT certifications out there which you can explore. However, the certifications from various companies listed in this section of the book are some of the most popular ones. Depending on the career you choose to settle for, these certifications will get you started and as you progress in the industry, you will learn more. Due to the dynamic nature of the ICT industry, most of these certifications would continue to change frequently. It is important to check online for the latest information regarding any of the certifications that interest you.

Other certifications include Apple, Avaya, C++ Institute, Citrix, CWNP, Esri (GIS professional certification), HP, Hitachi Data Systems, Huawei, IBM, ISECOM, iSQL, Juniper Networks, Linux, Redhat, Salesforce, W3Schools, VMware, and Zend Technologies.

For Tech trainings,videos and resources

Visit : www.iamadedoyin.com

Join or follow the conversation with the hashtag

#BeTechPro

SECTION 5

EMERGING TECH FIELDS

Artificial Intelligence

Artificial Intelligence, AI, is one of the fastest growing fields of technology right now. It is a part of tech that seeks to create intelligent machines to carry out a wide array of tasks with little or no human intelligence input. The goal of AI includes natural language processing (speech recognition and language translation), decision-making, reasoning, problem-solving, visual perception, learning and planning, moving and manipulating objects, knowledge representation, social and general intelligence, and creativity. Machine learning is what makes AI possible. Computers are fed with a large volume of information and are trained over time to build their own intelligence to understand properties, categories, objects, relations and patterns based on the information they are fed. Consequently, the computer continues to learn and build "artificial intelligence" with less supervision or human inputs. Artificial Intelligence is booming and increasingly being used in a lot of industries including finance, manufacturing, commerce and warehousing, security and healthcare. The use of AI will continue to grow in the next 10 years.

 3D Printing

3D printing, also known as additive manufacturing, is a process of creating a physical object from a 3D digital design. For example, I can design a unique phone cover using CAD software like AutoCAD, Tinkercad, SketchUp, Blender or FreeCAD. Once my 3D phone cover design is ready, I can send it to a 3D printer to print it out in plastic, glass or even metal. A lot of research and innovation is on-going to make 3D printers faster and cheaper.

The beauty of 3D printing is that it is changing manufacturing, construction and how we create new objects. 3D printing is increasingly having a lot of use in various industries. Today, a house can be designed on a computer and printed on-site by the machine within hours, and in medicine, body parts are 3D printed to solve a life-threatening situation, manufacturers can create prototypes of new products easily, custom machine part that could take weeks to manufacture are 3D printed. A lot is still ahead for the 3D printing industry.

Nanotechnology

There are a number of places where technology meets medicine. Nanotechnology is one of them. Nanotechnology uses science, engineering and technology to study and control very small particles to behave in certain ways or perform a task. It is an emerging field used across many science fields, such as chemistry, biology, physics, materials science and engineering. Technology plays a huge role in the success of Nanotechnology. If you are interested in innovative medical solutions using technology, this will be a very rewarding career path to follow. Nanotechnology continues to gain more attention and is used in many industries. As a result, the demand for Nanotechnology professionals will continue to grow.

 ## Robotics

.It is an exciting field of technology that needs to be paid attention. Artificial intelligence goes hand in hand with the robotics. This is because there is a strong connection between the two. We can say that artificial intelligence is the brain while robotics is the body; therefore, as the interest in artificial intelligence continues to grow so also will interest in robotics.

Robots are used increasingly in manufacturing and general utility services. The use of robots for domestic and industrial use will persist. There is an excitement about the future of robotics. Before long, homes, offices, factories will have robots executing various tasks. It will transform the way we live and work.

 ## Virtual & Augmented Reality

Virtual reality (VR) and augmented reality(AR) are computer technologies used to create simulated experiences. Virtual reality creates a 3D computer-generated world around you. For example, right in your home, you can simulate the peak of Mount Everest or what a walk in the desert looks like.

Augmented reality does not create a computer-generated environment like virtual reality. It creates virtual objects for your present environment; for example, you can have a virtual lion walking around or a virtual box of gold on your table.

Both AR and VR have a very interesting way of changing the perception of the world around us. A lot of industries are taking a significant interest in AR and VR. They will shape the future of the computer gaming industry, real estate, movies and cinemas, travels and tours, history documentation and more. There will also be an interesting integration of these technologies in mobile devices. AR is increasingly becoming an integral part of most Apple products while Sony and Samsung already have VR gadgets. The future looks interesting for VR and AR, that future is just getting started.

 Blockchain

If you are a regular internet user or you listen to the news, you probably heard of Bitcoin. Bitcoin is a digital currency that is online and can be used by anyone anywhere. Digital currencies or crypto-currencies seek to build a global digital financial system outside the existing banking system. This digital financial system would make transactions cheaper, faster and you don't have to worry about the difference in currency when doing business with someone in another part of the world. For this digital financial system to work effectively and track transactions, it runs on an open, distributed digital ledger that can record transactions between two parties efficiently and in a verifiable and permanent way. The technology behind this open ledger system is called blockchain.

The Blockchain is a decentralised and distributed digital ledger used to record transactions across many computers so that the record cannot be altered retroactively without the alteration of all subsequent blocks and the collusion of the network. Aside from digital or crypto-currency, blockchain technology is being considered for other uses like retail and commerce, medical records keeping, environmental management, identity management, transaction processing, agricultural management, elections and more. Right now, the use of blockchain for other industries is still at its infant stage. Hopefully, we will see more interesting solutions built from it. However, the idea and concept of the blockchain technology are already driving a change in how things are done in various aspects of the tech industry.

Internet of Things

In the last few years, the use of the internet has truly exploded. Every day, new ways of using the internet are being invented. The era of simply connecting computers and mobile phones to the internet is winding down, we are entering into an era where all electronic devices would be internet enabled and can be controlled via the internet. A good example is a smart home, which allows the house owner to control any part of the house via a mobile app. You can switch on and switch off light bulbs, check security camera feed, automatically open the front gate or door and do a lot more. Thousands of new devices are currently internet enabled; even, national infrastructures like the power grid, water supply, security camera and traffic lights are now connected to the internet.

The Internet of Things (IoT) is the network of devices, machines and other items embedded with electronics, software, sensors, actuators, and network connectivity which enable these objects to connect and exchange data. Each item is uniquely identified through its embedded computing system and is able to operate within the existing internet infrastructure. Internet of Things is opening new opportunities to a lot of industries such as the automobile, machine, energy, manufacturing and even customer products. It is an emerging field that holds particular promise for the immediate future.

On-Demand Services

The continuous evolution of technology is also rapidly changing how humans behave. Customer behaviour and needs are changing; companies around the world are changing their business models or building new businesses to meet these changes. One of those new business models is on-demand services. This is being able to meet the customer's needs exactly when they need it. A popular example is taxi booking. Today, you don't have to walk down the road to get a taxi; you can simply get a taxi in front of your house using a mobile app. The taxi mobile app tells you exactly when the taxi would reach you, the type of car and driver's details. There are also on-demand services available for food, shopping and a lot more. The on-demand services will continue to grow into other sectors and newer technology opportunities come up. Drones and artificial intelligence will play a huge role in the growth of on-demand services.

Automation

Most of the emerging fields of technology are heading towards one-point automation. A point where machines make decisions that normally would be made by humans. Almost every sector of the society would leverage automation in the coming years. Artificial intelligence, Internet of Things, robotics and more would usher us into the era of automation. Smart cars will drive themselves. Smart homes will know when to turn on the heater or switch off the light; you will order food and a drone will automatically deliver it to you within minutes; factories will have robots handling manufacturing none stop; medical devices will be able to give diagnostics and recommendations without human input; and traffic lights within a city will automatically readjust itself depending on the flow of traffic. There is an exciting future ahead for automation.

 Renewable Energy

Our climate is changing. We are beginning to witness extreme weather conditions across the world. Generating electric and mechanical power through coal and fossil fuel contribute to the damage of our atmosphere, which leads to extreme weather conditions. Consequently, there is a global movement to shift from the use of fossil fuel to renewable energy options which include solar, wind, geothermal, tidal waves and biomass. This global demand to change how we generate power is leading us to a new era of innovation. We are beginning to think about power differently. One of the biggest challenges of renewable energy option is that one source of energy cannot be available every time. For solar energy, the sun does not shine all day and for wind or tidal waves, we cannot control the wind or wave speed; therefore, there is a need for a hybrid power supply system or a smart power grid. This is where technology plays a vital role in the renewable energy industry. Smart grids are built to understand when to switch between various power sources to avoid a power outage. Technologies like 3D printing, artificial intelligence, Internet of Things and robotics continue to play a huge role in the rapid development of renewable energy. If you want to use your tech skills to change the world, renewable energy might just be the area to look into.

More countries are making serious commitments to renewable energy and green options. The opportunities ahead are huge for the industry and professionals.

For Tech trainings,videos and resources
Visit : www.iamadedoyin.com
Join or follow the conversation with the hashtag
#BeTechPro

SECTION 6

LEARNING OPPORTUNITIES ONLINE

Online Learning Platforms for Short Specialised Courses and MOOCs

One of the most beautiful things about this era is the unlimited availability of information. Technology has helped us to break barriers and offers learning opportunities beyond the traditional way of learning.

Online learning platforms are broadly grouped into two categories:
1. Platforms that allow skilled individual and professionals to sell courses on specific topics. These platforms enable skilled professionals to share their knowledge with the world for a fee. You can learn almost any topic on these platforms. Explore these platforms and learn something new. You will find very good ICT courses which would help you fast track your learning process.
Some of the most popular in this category include:
- Lynda.com owned by LinkedIn
- Udemy.com
- Khanacademy.com
- Skillshare.com

2. Platforms that offer Massive Open Online Courses (MOOCs) in partnership with academic institutions and technology companies. Today, top institutions around the world like Harvard University, MIT, Cambridge University, Oxford University, University of Melbourne and more globally recognised institutions have placed some of their courses, lectures and academic professionals on the internet. At the moment, you can access short courses from top universities across the world from the comfort of your homes without having to travel. You get certificates from taking some of these courses (usually at a fee). Also, the big technology companies are working with online learning platforms to offer specialised technology courses to bridge the growing need for skilled ICT Professionals.
Some popular platforms in this category include:
- Coursera.org
- EDX.org
- Udacity.com
- Codecademy.com
- Iversity.org
- Futurelearn.com

You can search online for MOOCs and learning platforms; there are more than 80 of these platforms to choose from depending on your need.

YouTube

With an average of 300 hours of videos uploaded every hour and 4 billion video views per day, YouTube is, no doubt, the largest entertainment empire on the internet. However, YouTube isn't just the about entertainment. I can say that it is the largest and most diverse online learning platform. The best part is that it is completely free and will always be available to you; all you need to do is search. Tons of videos are available on YouTube to enable you to learn anything you want to learn at any time. For technology professionals, there are several videos that can help you to teach yourself any ICT skill and also enhance your knowledge on the topic of your choice. Most of the ICT career and certification options are built around software. You will be amazed at the volume of awesome video lessons you can find on software on YouTube.

However, there are major downsides to YouTube as a learning platform:
1. Given the contents available on YouTube, you can easily get distracted. Therefore, it will take self-discipline and determination to ignore the distraction and focus on your learning objectives.

2. You can't really determine the skill level or professionalism of some of the curators of the YouTube videos you will watch. This is because it is open to everyone. This is in sharp contrast to the other standard learning platforms mentioned earlier, which brings some of the world's best professionals together to create quality video contents.

3. Locating a good video on a subject that interest you can be challenging. Even after searching, you will still need to review the results to try to see which one is good enough to meet your learning expectations.

For Tech trainings,videos and resources
Visit : www.iamadedoyin.com
Join or follow the conversation with the hashtag
#BeTechPro

SECTION 7

TIPS ON BECOMING
A TECH PRO

Discover Your Passion

Discovering your passion is a lot simpler than you think. Right from childhood our passion has naturally always played out in the things we choose to do; we just did not pay attention at the time. Most times, the journey from childhood to adulthood causes us to lose sight of that passion. Some are lucky to rediscover it later in life, but most lose it forever and settle for things they weren't designed for. Aside from God, there is nothing that can replace the joy and the lifetime fulfilment of spending your life doing what you love to do. It has a direct impact on the quality of life you will live.

To figure out what you are truly passionate about, you need to take some time out. Keep yourself away from the noise around you and focus on yourself; let your mind follow your curiosity.

You can try the following steps to help you reconnect with your hidden passion:

1. Think carefully about what you loved to do while you were a child. Try to remember the people you admired while you were young – what did these people do? Pick a sheet of paper and list those things in it.

2.   If you have an all-expense paid vacation for one month, what would you love to spend the one month doing? List them out in your paper.

3.   What are those things you can continuously do happily and without much effort whether money is involved or not? List them out in your paper.

4.   Sometimes, asking the people close to you questions about yourself can help you get more clarity. Ask them what they think you like to do. List them out in your paper.

Compare these four lists and see which items repeatedly show up on all the lists. This might be a pointer to your true passion.

While you search for your passion, it's also important to note that you have to distinguish between a hobby and a profitable passion. For example, if watching cartoons is on the list of things you love to do, that might just be a hobby which can point you to a profitable passion- digital animation. For those whose hobby is writing poems and stories, a profitable passion in line with this hobby could be a digital content creator. A profitable passion is that one thing that you can offer as a service to people and they are willing to pay for it. Spend time alone, ask yourself hard questions and meditate. The universe will always bring you answers.

The tech industry comes with a lot of opportunities and challenges. Tech professionals spend most of their time solving new problems, being innovative and seeking new ways to do things. It is passion and fulfilment that will keep you going on this path. Therefore, find your passion and start learning.

Start Learning, Don't Stop Learning, Keep Re-Learning

Once you have settled for a tech career based on your passion and personality, then the learning process begins. The internet is a good place to start; explore the internet to learn more about the tech career you have chosen. There is also a very good chance that there are online courses available for this career. To reduce the learning curve, it is better to start with introductory video courses or look for a tech training centre around you to learn the basics.

When you finally learn the basics, you can buy books, pay for more advanced courses and continue to learn. The beauty of tech is that there are tons of both free and premium resources for you to pick from. Tech professionals are lifetime learners, and being the best in your tech career is a continuous process. Technology keeps changing and reinventing itself at the speed of thoughts. Therefore, your passion has to continue driving you to keep learning and re-learning. As your professional experience grows, so also will your learning process. For most passionate tech professionals, they don't consider this learning but an adventure. It is an adventure to explore the unknown and achieve the impossible. To them, innovation is continuous. The thrill of the adventure and the determination to push back the boundaries of impossibilities drives them to keep learning and re-learning.

Self-Study Is How You Go the Extra Mile

About 85% of what you need to know to be one of the best in your tech profession will come from self-study and discovery. Self-study will play a significant role in your success in the tech industry. No training or online course will teach you everything because tech fields are elaborate. The best these training will do is to point you in the direction to go. By exploring and practising what you are learning, you will discover new possibilities and opportunities. Through self-study, you learn what works and the best options. The discoveries you make on your own will stand you out from others in the field. Aside discovery, self-study also helps you understand the relationship between your field and other tech fields. The more you dig in, the more you discover and the better you get professionally. This will translate into more rewarding opportunities for you.

The tech industry is rapidly evolving. The tools and software used are being updated almost every month with new features and additional functionalities. New tools or software would always emerge to change how things are being done in your field. It is continuous self-study that will keep you on top of your game. As you stay informed of the updates in software and tools, it will help you understand the trends in your profession. This way, you always have an idea of where your profession is heading.

Find a Tech Mentor

It is good to passionately explore the tech field and motivate yourself to continue to learn, but it is better to get a mentor that is experienced in that area. Having a mentor helps you cover a lot of ground within a relatively short time. Most mentors have been through some of the processes you are about to start, so they can easily guide you through the path. As a result, you make fewer mistakes and your learning curve is shorter. They also help you understand the current trends in your tech field. All these make it easier for you to know how to tailor your self-study and channel your developmental efforts to the right places. As you proceed on this journey, you will hit road bumps, but with a mentor by your side, it is a lot easier.

Another way to make the most out of having mentors is to have access to their network. Most tech professionals build a professional network of clients and colleagues over time. Needs would always arise within your mentor's network for your skill set and you can easily be recommended. I do suggest you get a mentor in a similar or closely related field to you. For example, if you want to be a computer programmer, find a computer programmer that can mentor you – the mentor might not necessarily have to use the same programming language as you. If you cannot find one in your field, then get a mentor in a closely related field like web design or development. One key issue with mentorship in the tech industry is that most experienced tech professionals are busy and may not have much time for you, therefore maximise the time they give to you. A way to get more time and learn from them is to volunteer to work with them on their existing project. This gives you hands-on experience to build your own portfolio to get opportunities in future.

Keep Asking Questions

"A traveller that is never tired of asking questions will never miss his way"– African Proverb
Asking questions is important on your journey to tech development. While you read and practice, you will always get to a point where you get stuck or you don't know how to achieve what you have in mind. Asking questions is one of the easiest ways to get past these stages. One of the most beautiful things about the tech industry is that it is a very large community of people that are always ready to help or share ideas and solutions with you. You will always find these communities in forums and discussion groups. By searching online, you can find these groups, forums or websites. There are very experienced tech professionals that devote their free time to supporting others and answering their questions. Sometimes, you will find that the question you have had been resolved in the past. By asking questions on these forums and groups, you can take advantage of the wealth of information of highly experienced people. Discussion

platforms like Stack Overflow and Quora have been very useful to me. On these platforms, you won't only get answers to your questions, but will also learn new things that you may not find in books or video tutorials.

When you ask questions, you get different answers and options on how to solve your problem. It will help you understand the different ways you can approach your task. Explore the web for groups and forums that are related to your tech field. Most of them are free; all you have to do is sign up and start making use of the wealth of experience available on these platforms. Once you sign up, you can go through past discussions. You will always find links to websites and resources that will accelerate your learning process thereby opening you to more possibilities.

Fail, Learn and Proceed

One concept I have developed over time in my tech journey and life is the concept of failing forward. The concept of failing forward is a self-assurance that I failed today not because I am inadequate or not smart enough, rather I did not just have enough information to understand that my plans won't work out. Failure in itself is not bad, what makes the ultimate difference is what you do with failure. You can allow it to crush your spirit, willpower and self-esteem or it can inspire you to keep your focus on your goal.

On your tech journey, you will fail a couple of times. Don't get discouraged, learn from it and keep moving. Sometimes, you will challenge yourself by embarking on a project that may be beyond your current capacity and you will make a complete mess of things. Sometimes, you won't be able to meet your client's deadlines or expectations. Learn from these low points and proceed with your journey. Where is the fun on a long journey if there are no bumps along the way? It is important to understand that you won't always win or get things right every time, rather learn the lessons and proceed. Always remember, quitters don't win and winners don't quit.
As a tech professional, you have more than enough support out there to get answers to your questions. What makes you a valuable professional in the tech industry is not just the things you know but your understanding of what works or doesn't. The way to know what works or doesn't is by continuously trying new thing; fail at some, learn from the failures and proceed to do things differently.

Keep Your Eyes on the Dream

"Dreams are like diamonds–they remain forever" – Unknown
Like anything worth doing in life – there will always be distractions and an aspiring career in tech is no exemption. Distractions will come in different forms. It could be your passion for something else which could take you away from your tech dreams. It could also be finances, relationship or pressures of life. As you step out to explore the tech world, you should have a dream of what you intend to achieve and over time create a roadmap on how to get there. Keeping your eyes on the goal (your dream) will help you remain in the game and avoid distractions on your tech journey. Keep your eyes on your dreams, keep learning and relearning, your winning moment is just ahead.

In addition to having a dream, you should always review and evaluate your 'tech' dreams. Innovations in this industry are happening at the speed of thoughts – your ideas of today might be irrelevant in the next six months. By continuous learning and understanding trends, you can always benchmark the growth and rapid changes in the industry with your dreams. This will help you see new ways of achieving your dreams or new possibilities to your dream. Let your ideas be flexible, not rigid so you can accommodate new possibilities to enhance the road map to your dream.

Don't let the potential size of an idea or dream scare you. No idea or dream is too big for you to achieve; rather, build your self-confidence, capacity and aim for that dream. "The future belongs to those who believe in the beauty of their dreams," says Eleanor Roosevelt. Don't let fear, doubt and distractions hold you back from going after your dreams. Write them down, paste it somewhere you can constantly see it and keep moving forward to bring it to reality. Aim for that big dream, be a history maker and like Norman Vincent Peale said, "Shoot for the moon. Even if you miss, you'll land among the stars". There are greater beauty and glory awaiting you on the other side.

Build Your Network
Often times I have heard motivational speakers say, "Your NETWORK is your NETWORTH". Beyond motivation, this is true for tech professionals. Having a resourceful network is very important for you in this industry. No sector of the tech industry is independent, every sector depends on each other to grow and innovate. Projects will come that will require you to look outside of your core tech field and

collaborate with other tech professionals. The larger your network, the more human and professional capital you have access to in your moment of need.

Building networks should not be limited to the tech industry; build networks outside the industry. It helps to enrich your view and exposure to things around you. Everyone wants to have a tech friend because they are considered smart and resourceful, use that to build connections outside the industry. As your influence grows within your network, you will get more referrals that will eventually grow your wealth and professional experience.

Building networks is a big challenge to some in the tech industry. Most times, we are consumed with our work that we don't pay enough attention to those around us. Tech professionals need to take some time off the computer to hang out with friends and family. It not only refreshes the mind, it also improves well-being. Some ways to build and improve your network include:

1. Take time off work to attend seminars, conferences, shows and exhibitions. Most of these events have sessions for networking. Be free and open-minded, meet new people and build friendships.
2. Join community projects. You can spend some of your free time doing projects within your community. It is a very good way to meet new people in your neighbourhood.
3. Explore tech hubs. Tech hubs are one of the few places you can physically meet diverse tech professionals. Tech hubs have had a good impact on me and the things I can do. You learn and share ideas across multiple tech sectors.
4. Meet your online friends, offline. You will always make new friends online. You can build better friendships with them by meeting them; spend some time together having a meal or a drink.

Building professional networks can have a huge influence not just on your tech career but also on your personality. While you continue to invest in developing yourself, put plans in place to build your network.

Jobs for Career Development

As a tech professional, there are two routes you have to take with regards to jobs. You are either self-employed, so you work as a tech freelancer and sometimes tech consultant, or you have a full-time job. Whichever route you take, they both have their merits and demerits but one thing is clear – there are a lot of opportunities available in the tech industry for those good at what they do.

For those seeking full-time jobs, getting a job is relatively easy. The challenge is picking the right job. While it is good to consider the salary and other benefits that come with a job offer, it should not be the only yardstick to determine which job to settle for. You should also consider a job that aligns with your career development plans and dreams. A job that pays well for your skill set and also gives you enough opportunities to develop your career is what you should choose. Let jobs be the stepping stone to your tech career development. It is also important for you to read the job description carefully to be sure it is a job you will enjoy doing. Career development is not easy when you are doing a job you don't like, your constant frustrations and anger with the job might end up killing your passion for your profession. After understanding what the job entails, it is important you research the company. Visit their website, search online, look out for news and reviews about them. All these will give you an idea of the company's culture and policies so you can determine if it aligns with your personal goals and objectives.

For those that choose the path of self-employment, you will have to develop extra skills with your tech skills; skills like interpersonal relationships, multi-tasking, problem-solving, basic accounting, project management and marketing. As a freelancer, you will deal with a lot of people with very different needs and it is important to think out of the box to solve their problems. Referrals are very powerful and will play a major role in your success as a freelancer. Ensure you deliver outstanding results to your clients so they can refer more clients to you. As you execute projects for clients, keep learning, develop yourself and explore new possibilities. The more problems you can solve, the more jobs you get and the better you get at solving these problems, the more you can charge for your services.

In all, a valuable tech professional is a problem solver, an innovator who keeps finding new ways of doing things.

For Tech trainings,videos and resources
Visit : www.iamadedoyin.com
Join or follow the conversation with the hashtag
#BeTechPro

SECTION 8

TECHNOLOGY FOR SOCIAL GOOD

"The real work is to discover who you are and to us who you are in service to the world" – Oprah Winfrey.

This quote had a profound impact on me when I first saw it some years back. I have since then used it as part of my signature for all my emails. One of the biggest issues with being a professional in the technology industry is that we usually get disconnected from the real world. This is because of the fast pace of the industry and the volume of work exploring technology can bring to you. Tech professionals just want to get lost in their digital world and shut out every other thing.

It would be a great disservice to humanity if I only show people how to get into the technology industry and not show them that tech professionals have the ability to impact humanity positively. It isn't enough for you to build a successful career, make money and live a comfortable life. You have the responsibility to use your technical skills to contribute to solving some of the biggest issues affecting humanity.

Technology for social good is a concept that seeks to use technology and innovation to solve various problems around us. Therefore, as you journey into the exciting world of technology, pay attention to issues around you, reflect on them, and think of how you can solve some of them with your technological skills. Paying more attention to the things around you with an open mind is like asking the universe questions; trust me, at the least expected time the universe will respond and point you in the right direction. You don't really have to leave your job to solve the issue; you can create some free time to develop a side project that addresses the issue. You can bring some of your friends together on Saturday afternoons to create solutions that can address specific needs in the world and make the world a better place. A technology for social good project can be a free software, web platforms that offer some services, a short film or documentary for an advocacy group or a photo-shoot that can be placed in a gallery for sale to raise money for people in need.

Technology is the biggest leverage we have in this generation to solve our problems and positively promote humanity. I hope as you continue on this path, you will find the balance between building an awesome career in technology and giving back to humanity.

Some interesting examples of technology for social good include:

1. Data Collection for Social Use

KoBoCollect is a free data collection Android app based on the Open Data Kit. It is used for primary data collection during humanitarian emergencies. With this app, you can enter data from interviews or other primary data -online or offline. There are no limits to the number of forms, questions, or submissions (including photos and other media) that can be saved on your device.

This Android app requires a free KoBo Toolbox account. Before you can collect data, create a free account using your computer on www.kobotoolbox.org and create a blank form for data entry. Once your form is created and active, configure this app to point to your account, following the instructions in the tool.

To visualise, analyse, share, and download your collected data, just go back to your KoBo Toolbox account online. Advanced users can also install their own KoBo Toolbox instance on a local computer or server.

KoBo Toolbox consists of several software tools to help you with your digital data collection. Together, these tools are used by thousands of humanitarians, development professionals, researchers, and private companies to design and implement primary data collection projects around the world. KoBoCollect is based on the Open Data Kit and is used by professionals wherever reliable and professional field data collection is needed. Data collected via this app can be transmitted to relevant agencies and government authorities to take quick actions that can save thousands of lives, especially during emergencies.

2. 3D Printing and Robotics for Amputees

Open Bionics creates cheaper prosthetic limbs – HERO ARMS
IMAGE CREDIT: OPEN BIONICS

3D scanning and printing are revolutionising how we create prototypes and new products across industries including Medicare. A number of tech start-ups use 3D printing to improve the lives of physically challenged people. With 3D scanning and printing, it is very easy to build braces, prosthetics and orthotics that specifically meet the need of a physically challenged person. One of the companies working in this sector is Open Bionics. Open Bionics is not just building 3D prosthetics; they are integrating robotics into their Hero Arm to make them truly functional.

According to the organisation, Hero Arm is the most affordable multi-grip bionic arm ever, less than half the price of its nearest competitor. Each Hero Arm is custom-built, and for the first time ever is available for upper limb amputees as young as nine. The world's first clinically tested, medically certified, and FDA registered 3D-printed bionic arm. Grab, pinch, high-five, fist bump, thumbs-up. Welcome to the future, where disabilities are superpowers. Open Bionics is building and developing the next generation of bionic limbs and turning disabilities into superpowers. Hero Arm is powered by space grade motors, advanced software and long-lasting batteries; it is lightweight and super sleek. Special sensors within the Hero Arm detect muscle movements, meaning you can effortlessly control your bionic hand with intuitive life-like precision.

3. Open Source Software

One of my favourite open source software is WordPress. WordPress started out as a blogging platform built with PHP and MYSQL. It has since evolved to become the world's most popular content management system. It is owned by Automattic and allows people to set up blogs where they can freely express themselves and communicate their thoughts to the world. The full codes used to build WordPress are freely available to download, install and use to build almost anything you want to build. Automattic generates their revenue from helping people manage their blogs as well as a number of premium WordPress related services while the open source version of WordPress has

104

been freely used by millions of people across the world to build online businesses. The open source version of WordPress has empowered a lot of people to generate revenue to take care of their families and needs. A company like Envato allows users to sell their WordPress themes and plug-ins; generating millions of dollars in sales for these people. A lot of businesses online are solely built to offer WordPress services. These businesses have generated a lot of revenue because of the huge community of WordPress users around the world. Recent statistics show that about 26% of websites globally are built using WordPress. The use of WordPress is vast and continues to date.

WordPress has empowered millions of people around the world socially, economically, politically and financially simply because Matt Mullenweg and his team at Automattic were passionate and courageous enough to release the WordPress code free to the world.

4. National Medical Deliveries using Drones

Zipline drone operating in Rwanda.
IMAGE CREDIT : CYRIL NDEGEYA/AFP/GETTY IMAGES

Medical deliveries using drones is one of the noblest Tech for social good idea I have come across. Zipline is doing it on a National level in Rwanda. According to the company's press release, in October of 2016, Zipline launched the world's first national drone delivery operation in Rwanda. The company was contracted by the Government of Rwanda to establish one distribution center with 15 drones to deliver blood, plasma and platelets to twenty one hospitals across the western half of the country. Since launching the service in Rwanda, Zipline has flown 300,000 km, delivering 7,000 units of blood over 4,000 flights, approximately a third of which have been in emergency life-saving situations.

The company is now delivering more than 20% of Rwanda's blood supply outside of the capital, Kigali. In addition to its impact on lifesaving emergency situations, Zipline's just-in-time drone delivery has helped transform the country's medical supply chain. To date, instant drone delivery has helped ensure that hospitals always have access to blood products, increasing the use of some blood products by 175% and reducing waste and spoilage by over 95%. Zipline is in the process of opening its second distribution center in Rwanda, which will help bring the entire country within range of its life-saving service.

For Tech trainings,videos and resources
Visit : www.iamadedoyin.com
Join or follow the conversation with the hashtag
#BeTechPro

SECTION 9

CONCLUDING NOTES

"Technology is nothing. What's important is that you have a faith in people, that they're basically good and smart, and if you give them tools, they'll do wonderful things with them." - Steve Jobs

Over the last few years, I have had the opportunity to train more than 1500 teenagers on Technology and Internet Usage. One thing I constantly mention in my training sessions is that we are one of the luckiest generations in history; to be alive when there are so much opportunities and potentials to do great things. Knowledge they say is power and we are in an era where access to almost any information is simply a push of a button. Thus it is safe to say, access to potential power is simply a push of a button. Today, technology has further broken down the boundaries of possibilities, connected the world like never before and created exciting new tools we can always leverage on to do great things.

Interestingly, Dr. Martin Luther King Jnr in his last historic speech – *"I've Been to the Mountaintop"* on April 3, 1968 in Memphis predicted this generation and the freedom that will be available to us to do great things.

Excerpts from Dr. Martin Luther King's speech
"And you know, if I were standing at the beginning of time, with the possibility of taking a kind of general and panoramic view of the whole of human history up to now, and the Almighty said to me, 'Martin Luther King, which age would you like to live in?' I would take my mental flight by Egypt and I would watch God's children in their magnificent trek from the dark dungeons of Egypt through, or rather across the Red Sea, through the wilderness on toward the Promised Land. And in spite of its magnificence, I wouldn't stop there.........."

"........ Strangely enough, I would turn to the Almighty, and say, 'If you allow me to live just a few years in the second half of the 20th century, I will be happy'. Now that's a strange statement to make, because the world is all messed up. The nation is sick. Trouble is in the land; confusion all around. That's a strange statement. But I know, somehow, that only when it is dark enough can you see the stars. And I see God working in this period of the twentieth century in a way that men, in some strange way, are responding. Something is happening in our world. The masses of people are rising up. And wherever they are assembled today, whether they are in Johannesburg, South Africa; Nairobi, Kenya; Accra, Ghana; New York City; Atlanta, Georgia; Jackson, Mississippi; or Memphis, Tennessee -- the cry is always the same: 'We want to be free'."

Today, Technology has given us that freedom Dr Martin Luther King talked about in 1968. The freedom to be whoever we want to be, learn anything we want to learn, go everywhere we want to go and build whatever we want to build. The only thing that can hold us down is our inner selves; everything we need is right before us irrespective of our race, location, colour or background.

As the information age winds down and usher us to a digital era, there will be a lot of uncertainty but one thing is sure – the coming era will make more exciting tools available for us to transform humanity for good. Technology will no longer be part of our lives, Technology will be our lives. It will shape our collective experiences and shared values.

Therefore, as Steve Jobs implied in his quote, we need more good and smart people to understand how to leverage the tools technology is providing to make a positive difference for humanity. There is great strength in numbers; we need more good and smart young people to explore innovation and technology for social good. This is my core purpose for this book – To help more young people understand the opportunities and power technology has given to them; to find their path in technology, develop themselves, build a successful career and leverage their skillset to solve global issues. As the digital era draws nearer, technology and innovation for social good is the platform we need a lot of young people to stand on to make a positive global difference.

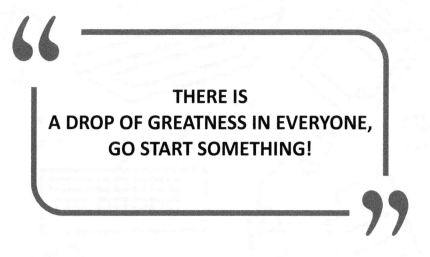

**THERE IS
A DROP OF GREATNESS IN EVERYONE,
GO START SOMETHING!**

www.ingramcontent.com/pod-product-compliance
Lightning Source LLC
LaVergne TN
LVHW051702050326
832903LV00032B/3958